DUBROVNIK

WARRINGTON BOROUGH COUNCIL	
34143100225356	
Bertrams	19/01/2010
AN	£7.99
WAR	

APA PUBLICATIONS

Part of the Langenscheidt Publishing Group

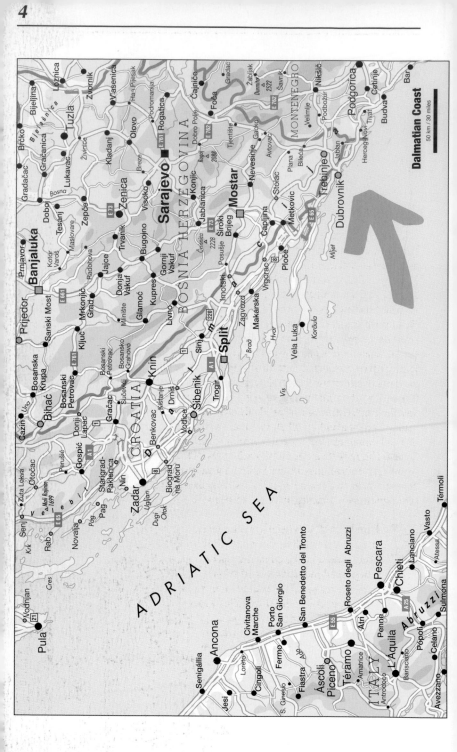

Dalmatian Coast

50 km / 30 miles

introduction

Welcome

This is one of 133 itinerary-based *Pocket Guides* produced by the editors of Insight Guides, whose books have set the standard for visual travel guides since 1970. With top-quality photography and authoritative recommendations, this guidebook brings you the very best of Dubrovnik in a series of 12 tours.

The former glittering Republic of Ragusa, and now a UNESCO World Heritage site, Dubrovnik has long attracted visitors. Half Roman, half Slavic, it grew as an outward-looking society, absorbing ideas from its various masters, Venice, Hungary and Austria, and developing its considerable native talent. Caught up in the Balkan conflicts of the 20th century, the walled city has emerged from their shadow and is once more welcoming visitors from across the world. This *Insight Pocket Guide* presents the best of the city in carefully designed itineraries for people with just a few days to spare, and suggests excursions to the surrounding coast and islands for those with a little more time. The first four itineraries concentrate on the historic Old Town, while two further walks explore the Ploče area to the east of the city and the Lapad peninsula to the west, followed by a boat trip to Lokrum, lying just off-shore. Five excursions then visit the Elaphite Islands and the idyllic coastal town of Cavtat, and venture slightly further afield: to Mljet, much of which is now a National Park; to Ston, where some of the world's finest oysters are produced; and to Korčula, home of the great stonemasons who built many of Dubrovnik's fine palaces. Supporting the itineraries are hotel and restaurant recommendations and sections on history and culture, nightlife and shopping, as well as a calendar of key festivals and a practical information section.

 Pam Barrett, who designed the itineraries, is a regular contributor to Insight Guide titles, with a background in modern European history and a love of of art, architecture, good food and sunshine, all of which come together in Dubrovnik. She hopes you will share her enjoyment of this lovely Croatian city, which blends a rich history with a vibrant modern outlook, and basks in a stunning setting beside the sparkling Adriatic Sea.

6 **contents**

HISTORY AND CULTURE

A brief history of Dubrovnik, from its 7th-century found-ation by the Illyrians, through the years when, as the Repub-lic of Ragusa, it was ruled by Venetians, Hungarians and Ottomans, to the 20th-century conflicts and its present sta-tus as part of an independent Croatia **11**

CITY ITINERARIES

Seven user-friendly tours, lasting from a few hours to a full day, explore the essential historical and cultural sights of Dubrovnik, two nearby peninsulas and the peaceful island of Lokrum.

1   Around the City Walls begins at the *Pile Gate* and takes a gentle walk along the top of the walls that encir-cle the Old Town, stopping off at the *Maritime Museum* and finishing with a visit to *Fort Lovrijenac* and the *Dance* church, just outside the enclave....................................**21**

2   Stradun and the Old Town Highlights runs down *Stradun*, the Old Town's main artery, visiting major historic buildings – the *Franciscan Monastery*, the *Sponza Palace*, the *Church of St Blaise*, the *Rector's Palace* and the *Cathe-dral* – en route. Stop for lunch in the *Old Port.* **25**

3   Around Prijeko is a short walk around the narrow, hilly streets north of Stradun, beginning with a visit to the *Dominican Monastery* and including the *Synagogue* and a moving museum of war photography **32**

4   Beneath the Walls runs through a quiet area of the Old Town and gives an opportunity to see neighbourhood life, as well as visiting the *Jesuit Church*, the *Rupe Ethno-graphic Museum* and an interesting *Icon Museum*.....**36**

5   A walk from Ploce Gate meanders gently past the *Lazareti*, the old quarantine station, offers a chance to stop on *Banje beach*, then visits the *Museum of Modern Art* before continuing along a rural road, with an optional trip to the *Museum of the Homeland War* on Mount Srd ...**39**

6   Lapad, Babin Kuk and Gruz The green and pleas-ant *Lapad* and *Babin Kuk peninsulas* are a short bus ride from the Old City, and close to *Gruz harbour*. This route will introduce the area and encompass a two-hour walk around the lovely Babin Kuk headland **42**

7   Lokrum Island takes a 15-minute boat trip to visit the remains of a *monastery*, explore the atmospheric *Botan-ical Garden*, and swim in a shallow saltwater lagoon called *Mrtvo More* (Dead Sea) **44**

Preceding Pages: the Old Town and the harbour
Following Pages: visitors outside Ploce Gate

EXCURSIONS

Five recommended excursions not far from the city. The first three involve pleasant boat trips, the last two are better done by road.

1   The Elaphite Islands The first and smallest of the three islands to be visited is *Koločep*, then comes sleepy *Šipan*, with *Lopud* usually left till last. This is the island with the most to see, including the remains of a monastery, a pretty harbour and a lovely sandy beach, *Sunj Bay*.................**47**

2   Mljet, much of which is now a National Park, is reached by catamaran in around 1 hour 45 minutes. The visit encompasses *Sveta Marija* (St Mary's Island) and two salt-water lagoons: *Veliko Jezero* (Big Lake) and *Malo Jezero* (Small Lake) **51**

3   Cavtat Take a trip by boat to this pretty village where you can visit the *Račić Family Mausoleum*; the house, now a *museum*, is where artist *Vlaho Bukovac* was born; and walk around the stunning coast **54**

4   Trsteno and Ston Visit the impressive *Arboretum* in tiny *Trsteno* about 18km (11 miles) up the coast from Dubrovnik and continue to the twin villages of *Ston* and *Mali Ston* to eat some of the best oysters in the world and to walk on the huge defensive walls **58**

5   Korčula is a lovely island, reached by boat or by road and a short ferry trip. This excursion suggests you concentrate on Korčula Town, where you can roam the narrow streets, visit St Mark's Cathedral and several interesting museums and leave time for lunch and a swim **60**

LEISURE ACTIVITIES

What to buy, where to eat, where to go and a guide to important occasions in Dubrovnik **67–79**

PRACTICAL INFORMATION

All the background information you are likely to need for your stay, with a list of hand picked hotels **81–92**

MAPS

Southern Dalmatia 4		*Lapad Peninsula* 42	
Dubrovnik **18–19**		*Elaphite Islands* **48–49**	
Old City **34–35**		*Mljet* **52**	
South of Stradun **38**		*Cavtat* **56**	
Ploče **40**		*Korčula* **62**	

CREDITS AND INDEX

pages **93–96**

History & Culture

For such a tiny place Dubrovnik has a fascinating history. Although its fortunes rose and fell along with those of the powerful neighbouring empires to whom it owed allegiance, it managed to retain a degree of autonomy and to steer its own course through troubled waters. While its defensive walls suggest that it was a city that could not be taken by force, in truth it was more often diplomacy and pragmatism that enabled Dubrovnik to retain its independence and to prosper economically. Today, as part of an independent Croatia, this beautiful city is putting the shadow of recent conflicts behind it and welcoming visitors with open arms.

Foundation and Security

The Dalmatian coast of the Adriatic has been inhabited since Neolithic times. By the 4th century BC, Greeks and Illyrians had taken up residence, only to be usurped, early in the 1st century BC, by the Romans, who established the colony of Illiricum. Although the Illyrians had been early converts to Christianity, the initial conversions of the Croats happened when Charlemagne, the first Holy Roman Emperor, conquered the area *c*. 800. Later that century, Cyril and Methodius, 'the apostles of the southern Slavs', brought Christianity to the masses.

Dubrovnik was an amalgamation of two settlements divided by a strip of marshy land that is now Stradun (the main street through the Old Town). The seaward settlement of Ragusa was established in the 7th century by Illyrians, fleeing from Epidaurum – modern Cavtat – after a disastrous attack, while the inland section, Dubrovnik (a name that derives from the Croation word *dub*, meaning holm oak) had been settled by Slavs over an extended period. The two became one when Stradun was paved over in the 12th century, and in 1181 it was first documented as the Republic of Ragusa.

Security was paramount in the minds of the early Ragusans. In 866 they were able to withstand a 15-month siege by Saracen invaders, which ended when they called on Constantinople for assistance and the Saracens left rather than put up a fight. Allegiance to Byzantium had proved beneficial but was of little help when, *c*. 999, Venice captured the Croatian coast, and the people of Dubrovnik were forced to submit to the Doge, Pietro Orseolo II. Venice was either not sufficiently powerful, or sufficiently interested,

Left: St Blaise holds a model of the city
Right: noble figure on the Sponza Palace façade

to enforce its will, and Ragusa was soon sheltering under Byzantium's wing once more. Twice during the 12th century Venice was to occupy Dubrovnik, but the city turned alternately to Norman and Byzantine rulers for protection, while still retaining much internal independence and building up strong trading relationships with its Serbian and Bosnian neighbours.

The Ragusan Republic was ruled by the aristocracy, headed by a rector. However, to prevent the office holder becoming too powerful, he was changed every month. Real power lay with the Grand Council and the Senate, with a Small Council as the executive body.

Venice Rules

It was at the beginning of the 13th century that Venice really made its presence felt. The Fourth Crusade, which began in 1202, ended with the Venetian and Papal armies sacking and looting Constantinople. Venice claimed half the city and installed a Venetian, Tommaso Morosini, as Patriarch. When Morosini demanded Dubrovnik's submission the ruling elite, realising that Byzantine power had waned, agreed to his terms. They had to accept a Venetian count as rector, take an oath of loyalty, offer hospitality to the Doge and his envoys, and provide assistance to the Venetian fleet in times of war. Most punitive was the tax the Venetians levied on all goods the Ragusans sold in Venetian ports, with the exception of perishable goods. On the other hand, Ragusa was allowed to trade in all the ports in which Venice traded, and was left alone, to a large extent, to run its own affairs. Throughout the 13th century, although Dubrovnik was involved in sporadic conflicts with neighbouring Serbia, it nevertheless succeeded in building a strong social and commercial structure.

During the 14th century, Dubrovnik cultivated good relations with Tsar Dusan of Serbia and his son, Tsar Stefan Uros V, from whom they were able to gain territory, including the island of Lestovo, Mljet and the Peljesac peninsula. The fact that this was done largely through negotiation boosted Dubrovnik's reputation for diplomacy.

Hungary and the Ottoman Empire

In 1358, under the Peace of Zadar, Hungary brought an end to Venetian hegemony over Dubrovnik and other Dalmatian cities, and Louis I of Hungary (1358–1433) became the new authority. The Ragusans were not too unhappy about this as they believed, rightly, that the Hungarians would not meddle much

Above: an idealised depiction of Ragusa
Right: a painting of medieval Dubrovnik

in their affairs. They were obliged to offer the usual allegiances, pay tributes and give assistance in wartime, but they were allowed generous trading privileges, and won the right to appoint their own rector, rather than accept one of Hungary's choosing. It was also during this period that the Republic made its final territorial gain – Konavle – although this region had to be fought for.

Then it was time for yet another switch of allegiances, this time to the Ottomans. In return for paying tribute, Dubrovnik was allowed to trade throughout the empire – a right that was confirmed by the Council of Basel in 1433, which gave Papal permission for trade with Muslim countries. This was to be advantageous for the Ragusan Republic during subsequent wars between Turks and Christians, when it was able to remain neutral and trade with both sides.

Religion and the Arts

Croatia has always been a predominantly Roman Catholic country. Even today, religious observance remains strong. St Blaise (Sveti Vlaho), a martyred Armenian bishop, became the patron saint of the city around the 9th century *(see page 10)*. The Benedictines, Dominicans and Franciscans all contributed to religious life, and many convents and monasteries were founded between the 9th and 14th centuries. The Jesuits arrived in the 1560s, but political wrangling saw them expelled then welcomed back several times over the next century.

The 15th and 16th centuries were a prosperous time, when the Republic flourished both commercially and artistically. Although the Dubrovnik School is not widely known outside Croatia, its artists produced a sound body of work. Much of their output was destroyed in the fire that followed the Great Earthquake of 1667, but some can still be seen. Three works by Nikola Božidarević (1464–1517) are in the Dominican Monastery Museum *(see page 32)*, which also displays a richly textured Baptism of Christ, by Lovro Dobričević (1420–78); his portrait of St Blaise is in the Franciscan Monastery and a polyptych in the Dance church. Another Baptism of Christ, this one by Mihajlo Hamzić (died *c.* 1518), can be found in the Rector's Palace.

Architecture also blossomed during the Italian Renaissance, spearheaded by Florentine Michelozzi; it was in the 15th century that some of the city's most splendid buildings were built or embellished. Most were destroyed by the earthquake, but the Rector's Palace and the Sponza Palace – harmonious blends of Venetian Gothic and Renaissance – have survived.

On the literary front, the two most influential writers were Marin Držić (1508–67), whose plays were revived in the 1930s and are still performed today; and Ivan Gundulić, who flourished somewhat later (1589–1638), and whose epic poem *Osman* was a cry of protest against Ottoman power.

Economic Upheavals

Thanks to the privileges Ragusa gained from her protectors, much of her wealth came from maritime trading. By the 16th century her fleet was extensive and the skill of her shipbuilders widely recognised. However, the good times did not last: the Republic's fortunes started to slide during the 17th century, when England and Holland became masters of the seas. In 1667 the Great Earthquake and subsequent fires devastated the city. The town was rapidly rebuilt, but its architectural and artistic treasures could not be replaced. In the 18th century there was an upturn in Dubrovnik's fortunes, but this came to an abrupt end when Napoleon occupied the city in 1806. Two years later he dissolved the Republic. Under the terms of the Congress of Vienna in 1815, Dubrovnik became part of the kingdom of Dalmatia and was ceded to the Austro-Hungarian Empire, of which it remained a part until 1918.

National Pride

With its independence gone, and Hungary's attempts at Magyarisation a source of discontent, Dubrovnik looked for a new source of pride, and found it, as oppressed people across Europe did in the mid-19th century, in romantic nationalism. The Illyrian Movement sought the unification of the Southern Slavs, and Ivan Gundulić became the nationalists' hero. Austro-Hungary was having none of it. Revolutions in Vienna and Buda in 1848 had been brutally represssed, and the imperial rulers were quick to nip Slavic nationalism in the bud.

However, the idea of political unity did not go away, although there were conflicting ideas about how it should be achieved. The National Party, led by Bishop Strossmayer, advocated a united Yugoslavia within the Austro-Hungarian Empire, while the Party of Rights, under Ante Starčević, called for a completely independent Greater Croatia. But independence had to wait. During World War I there was renewed pressure to unite the Southern Slavs, and in 1917 the Corfu Declaration outlined the structure of the future state. This

was confirmed by the Versailles Peace Treaty, and in 1919 the Kingdom of the Serbs, Croats and Slovenes came into being, with King Aleksandar at its head. It was not to be a happy union. Stjepan Radić (1871–1928), who had founded the Croatian Peasant Party in 1905, still hoped for an independent

Croatia. In 1928 a radical Serb MP shot Radić, who died from his wounds. The following year, Aleksandar abolished the Constitution, banned opposition parties, including the Ustace Croatian Liberation Movement, established a dictatorship and changed the name of the country to the Kingdom of Yugoslavia. In 1934 the king was assassinated in Marseilles by Yugoslav exiles, radical members of the Ustace.

War and its Aftermath

In 1941, two years into World War II, the Axis powers invaded Yugoslavia and installed the Ustace. Over the next four years the party massacred thousands of Serbs, as well as rounding up the Jewish population. Communist Party member Josip Broz (1892–1980), known as Tito, formed the Partisans, the main anti-fascist resistance movement. Realising that this group was the only force capable of ousting the Nazis, the Allied powers gave Tito their backing. He entered Belgrade at the head of the Red Army in 1944. When the war ended, the Socialist Federal Republic of Yugoslavia came into being, divided into six republics and two autonomous provinces, with Belgrade as capital and Tito as prime minister. In 1953 Tito was elected president and led Yugoslavia until his death.

During the Cold War years Tito kept Yugoslavia independent of the Soviet Union and outside the Warsaw Pact, and initiated the Non-Aligned Movement. He took steps to decentralise the economy, and, although the country's infrastructure had been devastated during the war, non-alignment meant that Yugoslavia could export goods to both Western and Eastern markets, and was able to open up, in the 1960s, to the lucrative tourist industry.

The Homeland War

Tito managed to keep a lid on the simmering tensions among constitutent parts of the state, but after his death in 1980 the discontent boiled over – fuelled by a failing economy and rising inflation. Slobodan Miloseviç took power in Serbia, and Albanians in Kosovo were brutally suppressed. Meanwhile, the election victory in 1990 of right-wing Franjo Tudjman at the head of the Croatian Democratic Union (HDZ) led to fears among Croatia's Serb community that they would be targeted. In 1991, encouraged by events throughout Eastern Europe after the the fall of the Berlin Wall, the Federal Republic broke up. Croatia and Slovenia both declared themselves independent states. Belgrade put up little resistance to Slovene secession, but bitterly resisted that of Croatia, and Serbs resident in the Krajina region proclaimed the Republic of Serbian Krajina. Hostilities – known as the Homeland War – broke out between Serbs and Croats, and thousands were killed. Dubrovnik was besieged

Left: monument to Gundulić, poet and nationalist hero
Above: Tito was president of the former Yugoslavia until his death in 1980

in October 1991, the port at Gruž and the airport destroyed, and the Old City subjected to mortar attack. Mainly because this was a treasured UNESCO World Heritage Site, and clearly not a military target, the European Union and the United Nations recognised the independence of Croatia and withdrew support and sympathy from the Serbs. Almost 100 civilians were killed in Dubrovnik during the siege and numerous buildings damaged, but a major reconstruction exercise has restored the city, which now shows few scars.

But peace had not been achieved. In 1995 the Croats took back areas of Slavonia and Krajina held by the Serbs, thousands of whom were forced into exile. Tudjman died in 1999; after a brief period of government by a centre-left coalition the HDZ returned to power in 2003, led by president Stjepan Mesić and prime minister Ivo Sanader – both less hard-line than Tudjman. Croatia now has its face firmly turned towards Europe and is expected to become a member of the EU in 2010. The conditions for membership are that they must co-operate with the UN war-crimes tribunal over electoral reform and the return of Serb refugees. A statement by the tribunal in March 2005 praised Croatia for its progress in this direction. The intricacies of the war and its aftermath, and relationships with Serbia, are subjects that are better avoided by visitors. The scars are too recent and too raw.

Today, the economy is still in poor shape, unemployment is high, and wages are low. But people are, generally, well-educated – Croatia's literacy rate is 97 percent – and members of the younger generation usually speak English. Medical care is good, and crime rates are low. People dress well, even on low incomes, and they like to go out and socialise. Dubrovnik has always been influenced by Italy, just across the water, and something of that country's flavour

remains today – and not just in the excellent pizza and ice cream.

Dubrovnik is rigthy proud of its stunning image and its World Heritage status and knows that these are its great selling points. Tourism is being nurtured as the major industry, although some do fear that the rapid growth of vast 'international' hotels and the number of cruise ships allowed into port, bringing tourist trade that is fleeting, intrusive and not lucrative for many except the port authorities, may change the character of the city. These are questions that need to be resolved, but there is a positive mood in the air, as can be detected in the evening flow of pedestrians along the Stradun, where little sign of the 1991 siege can be seen, and the city buzzes with optimism that the future will be less turbulent than the past.

Left: the Old Port in flames after bombardment in 1991

HISTORY HIGHLIGHTS

4th century BC Greeks and Illyrians are resident on the coast of Dalmatia.

1st century BC Romans usurp the earlier settlers and establish the colony of Illiricum.

395 After the division of the Roman Empire Southern Dalmatia comes under the rule of the western half, until its 5th-century collapse.

555 Dalmatia is conquered by Byzantine Emperor Justinian.

9th century Cyril and Methodius, 'the apostles of the southern Slavs', convert the masses to Christianity. Cyril invents the Glagolitic alphabet, in order to translate the Bible into the Slavonic language. St Blaise (Sveti Vlaho) becomes patron saint of the city.

999 Venetians capture Croatian coast for the first time.

12th century The settlements of Ragusa and Dubrovnik united when Stradun is paved over.

1181 First recorded mention of the Republic of Ragusa.

1202 Fourth Crusade. The Venetians demand the submission of Dubrovnik and install a Venetian as rector.

1358 Under the Peace of Zadar, Hungary gains control of Dubrovnik.

1433 Council of Basel gives Papal permission for Dubrovnik to trade with Muslim countries.

1508 Birth of playwright Marin Držić.

1560 Jesuits arrive in Dubrovnik.

1589 Birth of poet Ivan Gundulić.

15–16th centuries Dubrovnik School of painting flourishes.

1667 The Great Earthquake destroys much of Dubrovnik. Many great works of art are lost.

1690s Jesuit College and St Ignatius church are completed.

1806 Napoleon occupies the city. Two years later he dissolves the Republic.

mid-19th century Romantic Nationalist Illyrian movement seeks the unification of Southern Slavs.

1905 Stjepan Radić forms the Croatian Peasants' Party

1919 Under the Versailles Peace Treaty the Kingdom of Serbs, Croats and Slovenes comes into being, with King Aleksander at its head.

1928 Radić assassinated by a Serb MP.

1929 Aleksander sets up dictatorship; he calls it the Kingdom of Yugoslavia.

1934 Aleksander assassinated by members of the Ustace Croatian Liberation Movement.

1941 Axis powers invade Yugoslavia and install the Ustace in power.

1941 Tito enters Belgrade at head of Red Amy, backed by Allied powers.

1945 Socialist Republic of Yugoslavia comes into being.

1953 Tito elected president. Initiates Non-Aligned Movement and decentralises the economy.

1960s Tourist industry flourishes.

1980 Death of Tito.

1979 Dubrovnik declared a UNESCO World Heritage Site.

1990 Franjo Tudjman elected president, at the head of the Croatian Democratic Union (HDZ).

1991 Break up of Federal Republic.

1991–92 Homeland War. Dubrovnik besieged.

1990s Rebuilding of damaged city goes ahead. Gruž port and Čilipi airport are rebuilt and tourist industry flourishes.

1999 Death of Tudjman.

2003 HDZ returns to power under more moderate president Stjepan Mesić.

2005 Croatian general Ante Gotovina arrested in December for mass murder of Serb civilians in 1995.

2008 March: Gotovina goes on trial; proceedings expected to last 14 months.

history/culture

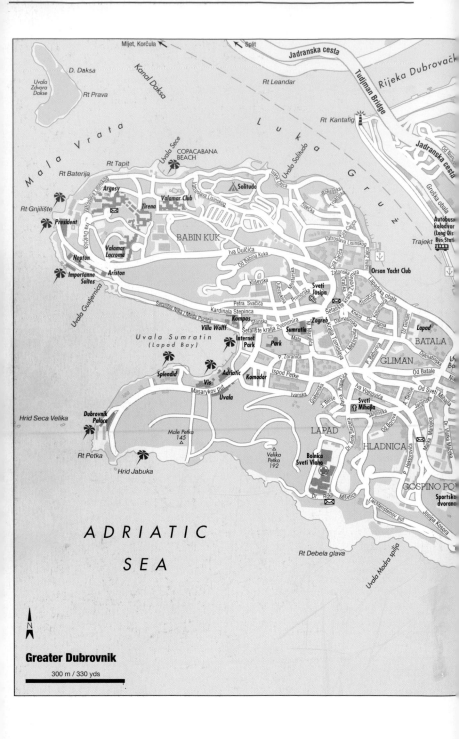

Greater Dubrovnik

300 m / 330 yds

CROATIA

Brač
Makarska
Hvar
Šćedro
Vis
Biševo
Vela Luka
Korčula
Pelješac
Korčula
Sušac
Lastovo
Mljet

Široki Brijeg
Ljubuški
Mostar
Plužine
Čapljina
Ploče
Metkovic

BOSNIA HERZEGOVINA

Ljubinje

Bilečko jez
MONTE-NEGRO

Trebinje

Dubrovnik
Zvekovica

Herceg Novi

ADRIATIC SEA

50 km / 30 miles

NUNCIJATA

Strinčjera
412

Gruž
Petka
GRUŽ
Metohijska
Sustjepana
Perice Padre
A. G. Matoš
Autobusni kolodvor
(Libertas Bus Station)
Robna kuaa
Stadion
ŠPČINE
Dr. Ante Starčevića
Put Republike
DONINOVO
Rajčevića
NTOVIERNA
Youth Hostel
Lero
P. Čingrije
Bellevue
Libertas
stan Svete lji muzej
htensteinov put
Vlaha
Put Republike
Jadranska cesta
Gornji Kono
Od Celja
Andrije Hebranga

GORNJI KONO

N° Nodila
Vladmira
SREDNJI KONO
Nazora
Petra Bakića
Zagrebačka
Anice Bošković
Branitelja Dubrovnika
B. Bogišića
Pera Budmanija
Srednji Kono
Šalve
Gornji Kono

PILE

Uvala Danče
Rt Gospa
Sv. Danač
PARK
Hilton Imperial
Inter-University Centre
GRADAC
Rt Danče
Rt Zudio

Srd
403
Muzej Domovinskog rath
(Museum of the Homeland War)

Jadranska cesta
PLOČE

Anta
Topica
M. Minges
Bura Bojića
Stainica

Uspinjača (Srd)
Petra Krešimira IV
Franjevacki samostan-muzej
M. Perica Hvarska
Dominikanski samostan-muzej
Lazareti
Kaše
Moderna Galerija
Excelsior
BANJE BEACH

Etnografski muzej Rupe
Džamija
Dubrovacki musej
Stara Luka
Rt Porporela
Tvrdava Sv. Ivan

Tvrdava Lovrijenac
(Fort Lourijemac)

STARI GRAD
(WORLD HERITAGE)

Cavtat

Placa
Stradun
Prijeko
Od Puča

City Itineraries

1. AROUND THE CITY WALLS *(see map, pages 34–35)*

One of the best ways to start a visit to Dubrovnik is by taking a walk around the City Walls, to get a feeling for the layout and the history of the city. This route also includes a visit to the Lovrijenac Fortress and DančE church, just outside the walls, as well as a suggested seafood lunch and a swim.

Start outside the Pile Gate, where buses deposit visitors from the hotels in Lapud, Babin Kuk and Gruž. The No 6 and No 4 are the most useful bus routes – No 6 is the more frequent (see page 84). Start relatively early if you can, to avoid the midday heat and the tour group crowds. Remember a hat and sunblock, but you can get refreshments on the way round, and you can leave the walls and return at other entrance points as long as you hold on to your ticket. Don't forget a film for your camera.

There is usually a bit of a scrum outside the **Pile Gate**, as passengers, disgorged from tour group buses, stop on the ancient drawbridge to take photographs of the patient young men in the ceremonial costumes of the Ragusan Republic who guard the impressive external gate (10am–noon and 8–10pm). Above it all a figure of **Sveti Vlaho** (St Blaise), the city's patron, holding a model of Dubrovnik, looks down with a benign expression. Through the gate and down a few steps is the inner gate, and immediately to the left, inside the fortifications, is one of the three entrances to the **City Walls** (open 8am–7pm; entrance fee, which also gives admission to the Lovrijenac Fortress). The best reason for starting the circuit here is that, if you go round in a clockwise direction, you get the steepest part of the walk over with first, while you are still fresh. After that, it is fairly flat and easy.

Northern Views

As you climb the long flight of stone steps you look down, first, on the roofs and cloister of the **Franciscan Monastery** *(see Route 2)* before reaching the highest point on the walls, the **Minčeta Fortress**, designed and built, like the Rector's Palace, by Italian architect Michelozzo Michelozzi and Dalmatian Juraj Dalmatinac, and with views that make it well worth the climb. As you continue along the north side of the city, all the views are breathtaking, and you will probably have to negotiate your way around other visitors taking photographs. Looking down on the terracotta rooftops, only the shiny newness of some of the tiles indicates that the originals were shattered by shell and mortar fire from the ridge, looming above you on the other side.

Left: church and cathedral stand almost side by side
Right: the city patron, St Blaise, keeps watch above Pile Gate

A short way along there is a hole-in-the-wall refreshment kiosk, and at the next (smaller) fortress, **Sveti Jakova**, sits a photographer who, for a small fee, will superimpose your picture onto a view of the city. Below are the rooftops of the **Dominican Monastery** and its Gothic-Renaissance bell tower. Begun in 1390, this tower, with its two great bells, dominates the city, although it faces stiff competition from the **Cathedral**'s lantern dome and the great bulk of the **Jesuit Church**.

Rounding a bend in the walls, your views out to sea are over the **Revelin Fortress**, the **Lazareti** and the coast stretching down towards Cavtat. To your right, you look down on the rear of the ancient churches of St Nicholas and St Sebastian, before reaching the **Ploče entrance** to the walls where you can, if you wish, descend to ground level to visit the port and continue the walk later.

The Harbour and Maritime Museum

Follow the walls now above the harbour, busy with the traffic of small craft coming and going to Cavtat and Lokrum, and round the far side to the **Sveti Ivan Fortress**, which houses the **Pomorski Musej** (Maritime Museum; open Tues–Sun 9am–6pm; entrance fee). Laid out over two spacious floors the cool, air-conditioned museum gives an interesting glimpse into the history of this maritime city. There are models of 16th-century carracks and galleons, an illuminated view of the port before the Great Earthquake of 1667 (the original painting is in the Franciscan Monastery collection), pictures of 19th- and early 20th-century steamships and their masters, and photographs of boats burning in the harbour during the 1991–92 siege.

South of the City

Setting out along the south side of the walls you reach the **Sveti Spasitelj Fortress** (where there are public toilets). To your left you have a great view of the island of **Lokrum** *(see page 44)*; to your right you look down on a patch of ruined walls and rubble, the result of an earthquake in 1979. Lack of funds and the subsequent devastation of the Homeland War have left this area unrestored. If you look ahead you will see, pinned to the outer wall of the next fortress (**Sveti Stjepan**), a figure of St Blaise, and perhaps wonder how he was manoeuvred and fixed in this seemingly precarious position. At the next fortress (**Sveti Margarita**) there's a café and, to your right, a view of the Jesuit Church *(see page 37)*, a neat vegetable garden and,

Above: Stradun and the Clock Tower
Right: tending a city vegetable garden

a short way on, a chapel to the rear of St Mary's Convent. From now on there's nothing but the sea to your left and, to your right, a glimpse of the everyday life of Dubrovnik, with narrow houses, carefully tended, flower-filled gardens and children playing ball. Then, after passing above another patch of ruins dating from 1979, you reach the **Bokar Fortress**, with views over Fort Lovrijenac on the headland. The circuit is complete. Descend to street level now, and back out of Pile Gate.

Fort Lovrijenac

This walk will probably have taken you 1½ to 2 hours, so you may now feel like sitting on the large terrace of the Kavana Dubravka in a square overlooking a little bay, and having a cool drink before you go any further. Stalls are set out in the square with handicrafts for sale. If you are hungry, the **Nautika** restaurant opposite *(see page 73)* does a 'light lunch' from noon to 4pm. The next stage of the route takes you down Svetoga Durda, the narrow alley beside the square, past a branch of the Atlas tour agency. You reach a tiny chapel (Sv. Durda) at one side of Brsale bay, where there's a little fishing jetty. The Orhan Restaurant (to which we shall return) sits on the other side of the bay, at the foot of 165 steps which must be climbed to reach **Fort Lovrijenac** (open 8am–7pm; entrance fee or admittance with City Walls ticket). Above the entrance to the fortress an inscription reads 'Non Bene Pro Toto Libertas Venditur Auro' (Freedom should not be sold for all the treasure in the world). This massive, early 16th-century structure was regarded as vital to the defence of the city, and its commander, like the Republic's rectors *(see page 12),* was changed on a monthly basis to prevent an opportunist gaining a power base and staging a coup. The leaders of the Ragusan Republic, it seems, were cautious to the point of paranoia. The fort is sometimes the venue for performances of *Hamlet* during the Summer Festival (July–Aug). A more dramatic setting for the tragedy would be hard to imagine.

The Danče Church

Back down the many steps now for a well-deserved lunch on the vine-clad terrace of the **Orhan Restaurant** *(see page 74).* If you come at the weekend, it's advisable to book in advance. Afterwards, follow the narrow road called

Above: Bokar Fortress and Brsale bay

Od Tabakarije through a pretty little neighbourhood and up a hill. Ahead of you, where the roads Frana Bulića and Dante Alighieri meet, stands an imposing building belonging to the Dubrovnik University. Turn left and follow the road through a car park atop a headland, then down a pine-shaded slope where the air is scented with herbs.

You will soon reach the Franciscan **Convent and Church of Danče**, built on the site of a medieval leper colony. There is a well-tended garden here and a little cemetery (originally the last resting place of paupers and convicted criminals). The convent is still a functioning one and there are usually nuns around who will let you into the church, but this cannot be guaranteed. The main reason to come here is to see the Lovro Dobričević polyptych (1465) above the altar, one of only three of this artist's works to have survived. Respect the nuns' silent prayer and meditation, and remember to drop a little something in the donations box to the right of the door before you leave. If for any reason you can't gain access to the church, your journey will not have been wasted, because it is a peaceful and beautiful spot, filled with the sound of birdsong.

Journey's End

From here, you could follow the example of many local people and take the path down to the cove below, a popular swimming spot. Or you can go back up to the car park and turn left, to find yourself in a shady and usually empty park – Gradac – where there is a small fish pond and fountain, benches set beneath the trees, and far-reaching views out to sea. On a headland up the coast, in the Boninovo district, the huge Hotel Libertas, destroyed with considerable loss of life in the 1991–92 Homeland War, has now been rebuilt, and stands close beside the newly renovated Hotel Bellevue.

From the park, follow Frana Bulića back to the university and take the right-hand fork down Dante Alighieri (the poet's bust sits on a plinth at the far end). You could stop for drink at **Sesame**, a pleasant café in an old family house that's popular with students (there is also accommodation available), before reaching the busy main road, whose name, along this stretch, has recently been changed to Branitelja Dubrovnika, which means Defenders of Dubrovnik. Here a right turn takes you downhill past the tourist office, with the smartly renovated Hilton Imperial opposite, and back to the Pile Gate and the bus stops where you began.

Above: city rooftops, old and new
Right: Stradun looks lovely even in the rain

2. STRADUN AND OLD TOWN HIGHLIGHTS
(see map, pages 34–35)

The highlights of the Old Town (Stari Grad) can be seen in a day, with a stop for lunch, but could be spread out over two days if you want to pace yourself and avoid getting saturated with museums and churches. Some places close on Monday, but most open every day in summer.

As with the previous route, start outside the Pile Gate, where you could stock up on bus tickets from one of the newspaper kiosks, or from the office of Libertas, the bus company, if it's open.

Across the drawbridge and through the outer and inner gates, you are faced with the glistening, marble-paved stretch of **Stradun**, also known as **Placa**, the Old Town's main artery. Immediately to your right is the domed 15th-century **Large Onofrian Fountain**, named after the Italian engineer, Onofrio della Cava, who masterminded Dubrovnik's first mains water supply. A strolling minstrel here poses for photos for a small fee and tourists and teenagers share space on the broad steps. Behind the fountain is the huge cloister of **St Clare's Convent**, which now houses the Jadrun restaurant, whose considerable size makes it popular with tour groups.

The Franciscan Monastery
On the left-hand side of Stradun, by the entrance to the **City Walls** *(see Route 1)* is the **Sveti Spas** (Church of Our Saviour), which is often closed in the day but is the venue for chamber music concerts on Sunday, Monday and Wednesday evenings in summer *(see page 78)*. Next door is the **Musej Franjevačkog Samostana** (Franciscan Monastery and Museum, open daily 9am–6pm; entrance fee). On your left, inside the main entrance, is a delightful old – but still functioning – **pharmacy** (open 7am–7pm, Sat 7.30am–3pm) with ornate shelves and ceramic jars. Then you step into the beautiful Romanesque-

Gothic cloister, where capitals on the slender columns are decorated with human and animal figures and floral motifs. These survived the Great Earthquake of 1667, which damaged the monastery and church, and the 19th-century depredations when both French and Austrian troops were barracked here at different times and used the cloister to stable their horses. Frescoes depicting the life of St Francis and his arrival in Dubrovnik decorate the walls; in the centre, where herbs for the original pharmacy used to be grown, a statue of the saint stands on a fountain.

Within the museum are some fine paintings, among which a 15th-century polyptych featuring St Blaise, by Lovro Dobričević, stands out. There is also a collection of reliquaries and chalices and some splendid 15th-century illustrated manuscripts. In the pharmacy section, reinstated in its original position, ancient jars, bowls and implements are displayed. The monastery was hit by numerous shells during the 1991–92 siege, and the hole pierced in the wall by one missile shot has been preserved behind glass.

You pass from the monastery into the **church** (open 6.30am–noon, 4–7.30pm; free if entered from the street), where the altars are baroque replacements for those destroyed in the 17th-century earthquake. Above the main one is a fine marble *Christ Resurrected* by Ivan Toschini (*c.* 1712), and the altar of Anthony of Padua is surrounded by a delightful painting by Ivo Dulčić (1916–75), installed here in 1962. To the left of the main altar a plaque commemorates the revered poet Ivan Gundulić (1589–1638), who is buried here. Best of all, however, is the *Pietà* outside, above the main (south) door – a lovely, soulful piece that managed to survive the earthquake and subsequent fire.

Stradun and Luža Square

Back in the bustle of Stradun is the Festival Café – cosy and wood panelled within, shady without – which serves excellent sandwiches. Although it gets crowded when cruise ship groups are being shepherded around, Stradun is a great street to stroll along; you can admire the uniform curved doorways and green shuttered windows of the elegant buildings, and watch reflections dance in the mirror-like surface of the street. There are two good bookshops, a small gallery or two, and a couple of shops selling high-quality clothes, but

souvenir shops, featuring Dubrovnik T-shirts, sunhats, fridge magnets and key rings are increasingly making their presence felt.

It's not a long street, and soon you reach the far end, Luža Square, where **Orlando's Column** stands in the centre, as it has since 1418. Orlando is also known as as Roland, as in the *Chanson de Roland*. The story linking him with the defence of Ragusa in the 9th century is without any foundation whatsoever, and chronologically impossible, but he has become a much-loved symbol of freedom. State declarations used to be read from the platform above the statue and condemned criminals exhibited at the base, *pour encourager les autres*. Straight ahead of you as you stand at Orlando's feet is the great **Clock Tower**, its bell chimed by the hammers of little green men, and with a rather anachronistic digital clock below. Beneath the clock, to the right, is the **Small Onofrian Fountain**, designed, like the larger one, by della Cava, a pretty little creation, popular with pigeons and as a backdrop for tourists' photographs.

Sponza Palace and St Blaise

To the left is a rare survivor of the 1667 earthquake, the **Sponza Palace** (usually open all day but sometimes inexplicably closed; free), with the single word *Dogana* on the metal studded door indicating that this used to be the customs house. This is a beautiful building, the delicate windows Venetian Gothic, the main doorway and upper floor late Renaissance, designed by Pasko Miličević and executed by the Andrijić brothers, the renowned Korčula stonemasons *(see pages 61–62)*. Inside you can admire a narrow, galleried courtyard, and see the original mechanism from the Clock Tower standing rather forlornly at the end, but leave time to visit the **Memorial Room of the Defenders of Dubrovnik** (open 10am–4pm; free) to the left as you go in. Here, photos of those who died in the 1991–92 siege, many of them heart-rendingly young men, are positioned around the walls. Above them are pictures of burning boats and buildings, while a video plays scenes of devastation.

Back in the square the **Church of Sveti Vlaho** (St Blaise; usually open 8am–noon, 6–8pm, but times vary; free) is a baroque structure with an interior that is relatively restrained. As the church of the city's patron it is a favourite place for weddings and baptisms. Within, there's an early 18th-century *Martyrdom of*

Left: the shady cloister of the Franciscan Monastery. **Above:** cooling off in the Small Onofrian Fountain. **Right:** the metal-studded door of Sponza Palace

city itineraries

St Blaise on the organ loft and, on the main altar, a silver statue of Blaise holding a model of the city, which shows what it looked like before the earthquake. The fact that this was the only statue in the church to survive the tremor was taken as evidence of the saint's powers. The stained-glass windows, depicting saints Peter and Paul, Cyril and Methodius, are by Ivo Dulčić (1916–75), one of Dubrovnik's most renowned modern artists *(see below)*.

To the left of the church are the imposing buildings of the **Gradska Vijećnica** (Town Hall), the ornate red-and-gold **Marin Držič Theatre** and the **Gradska Kavana** (Town Café), within the arches of the old arsenal. With a cavernous interior and broad terraces facing onto the square and the port on the other side, the Gradska Kavana is a Dubrovnik institution. It has recently been renovated and expanded to include the adjoining Arsenale Restaurant and Wine Bar, and the first-floor Sloboda Cinema, which shows many Hollywood movies in English, as well as Croatian films.

Lunch in the Old Port

This would be a good time for a midday break. You could get a light lunch in one of the cafés at this end of Stradun, but it's better to go through the gateway between the Sponza Palace and the Clock Tower to the **Old Port**, where you have a choice of two restaurants. **Poklisar**, on the left, close to the stalls selling tickets for boat trips, is a big, cheerful place serving pizza and fish dishes under a striped awning. Round the corner, past women selling – and making – crocheted and embroidered cloths of various kinds, is the best choice, the **Lokanda Peskarija**, an unpretentious little place with tables

Above: altar and organ in the Church of St Blaise

city itineraries

spreading out across the jetty, that serves excellent and inexpensive seafood *(see page 72)*. Both places have glorious views of the harbour, the coast-line, and the constant coming and going of small boats. Alternatively, you could go to the popular Kamenica in Gundulić Square *(see page 31)*.

The Rector's Palace

Back in the square, the next on the left is the **Knežev Dvor** (Rector's Palace) which will re-open in 2009 after renovations (check for hours when you arrive). The two earlier versions of the palace – the second of which was designed by Onofrio della Cava, who built the fountains – were both destroyed in fairly quick succession in the 15th century by gunpowder explosions in the nearby arsenal, an expensive example of not learning from experience. The current palace, incorporated into the remains by Florentine Michelozzo Michelozzi (1396–1492), has a stunning loggia with intricately carved cap-itals – both Gothic and Renaissance – atop pillars of Korčula marble. One of the figures on the far right capital is thought to represent Aesculapius, the god of healing. Inside, the atrium, also a harmonious mixture of Gothic and Renaissance, is the venue for Summer Festival events and for regular concerts by the Dubrovnik Symphony Orchestra throughout the summer. The acoustics are excellent, and it is a magical setting in which to hear music on a summer's night. The bust in the centre commemorates Miho Pracat, the Lopud merchant and mariner who left his entire estate to the Republic *(see page 49)* and was the only commoner immortalised in this way (Gun-dulić, whose statue we shall see shortly, was a nobleman). Confusingly, the Italian version of Pracat's name – Michaeli Prazotto – is given on the statue.

Visiting the museum, you are directed to the right, through a room containing 16th-century portraits, mostly unattributed, then into the Court Room where there are explanations, in English, about how the court functioned during the Republic. Stairs lead down to a vaulted room where there are excellent por-traits of Ivan Gundulić and of mathematician Marin Getaldić (1568–1626), friend and contemporary of Galileo, who conducted experiments in a cave not far from the Ploče Gate *(see page 39)*. Adjoining this room are the former prison cells, with carved wooden chests and statuary, including a 15th-century St Blaise from the palace doorway. Back in the atrium, you ascend the wide staircase, where the wooden handrail is supported by huge stone hands, to visit the splen-did reconstructed staterooms, with mullioned windows overlooking the street and Cathedral. The Republic's rectors, each elected for only one month at a time to prevent them get-ting too uppity, were not allowed to leave the palace during their period of office or move their families in with them, but at least they lived in

Right: a helping hand in the courtyard of the Rector's Palace

comfort. The Rector's Study (complete with a red-robed model rector) displays a lovely *Baptism of Christ* (1509) by Mihajlo Hamzić.

The Cathedral

Back in the street, you could rest in one of the padded rattan armchairs outside the **Hemingway Bar** and have a cool drink before visiting the imposing, lantern-domed **Cathedral** (usually open 8am–8pm; free; small entrance fee for Treasury). The original Romanesque building, said to have been financed by Richard the Lionheart after he was shipwrecked on Lokrum *(see page 44)* was destroyed, like so much else, in the 1667 earthquake. Its baroque replacement, the work of Italian architects Andrea Buffalini and Paolo Andreotti, completed in 1713, is surprisingly simple, although the side altars are somewhat overblown. Above the severe lines of the modern, marble altar (the earlier one was destroyed in another earthquake in 1979) is a School of Titian polyptych.

The **Treasury**, to the left of the altar, is tiny, and packed with revered objects. Chief among them are an enamelled gold reliquary of St Blaise's head, and reliquaries in delicate gold and silver filigree of his arms and one leg, which are carried in procession around Dubrovnik on the saint's day, 3 February *(see page 78)*. Numerous other reliquaries are kept here, as is a copy of Raphael's lovely *Madonna della Seggiola* (the original is in the Pitti Palace in Florence). These treasures were first kept in St Stephen's Church, taken to the Revelin Fortress after the 1667 earthquake, then moved to the Dominican Monastery before being brought here on St Blaise's day in 1721.

Contemporary Art

Opposite the Cathedral, built into the city wall, is the **Galerija Dulčić-Masle-Pulitika** (open Tues–Sun 10am–8pm; entrance fee), a small gallery dedicated to three local artists: Ivo Dulčić (1916–75), whose stained-glass windows you can see in St Blaise's and mosaic altarpiece in the Dominican church; Antun Masle (1919–67), some of whose work is also in the Dominican monastery's collection; and Duro Pulitika , who lived in Dubrovnik until his death in 2006 at the age of 84, and whose delightfully simple *Holy Family* hangs in the Dominican church. The col-

lection, and the changing exhibitions, are small but worth seeing if you are interested in contemporary art. You will probably notice the influence of these artists on many of the paintings in small private galleries around the town.

The gallery (also accessible from the top of the walls) is housed on the upper floors of the **Ronald Brown Memorial House**. Brown, the first African-American US Secretary of Commerce, was the leader of an American trade delegation to Croatia whose plane crashed on the mountainside above Cavtat in 1996 *(see page 56)*. You can peep into a room to the left of the entrance, where photographs of Brown and the 34 people who died with him, along with a roll of honour, are displayed, but the door is rarely open.

Left: a graceful modern sculpture
Above: art gallery sign, opposite the Cathedral

Gundulić Square

Go round the back of the Cathedral now, and you will find yourself in Buničeva Poljana, a square full of café tables – and, at night, usually full of noise and music, as it's a popular meeting place. On one corner is the **Jazz Caffé Troubador**, where live jazz is played most evenings. This square leads into another, larger one, **Gunduličeva Poljana** (Gundulić Square), named after the 17th-century writer who symbolised Croatian national identity, not only in his own time, but again during the 19th-century nationalist revival and the conflicts of the late 20th century. His statue stands on a plinth in the centre of the square, a handy perch for the resident pigeons, who show him no reverence whatsoever.

Gundulić Square has two separate identities, depending on the time of day you come here. In the morning it is the setting for a lively local market, full of colourful fruit, vegetable and flower stalls, together with a few offering embroidered linen, herbs and lavender water. By 1pm, there is scarcely a sign left of this activity, and tables, chairs and sun umbrellas are set out by waiters from a line of restaurants that include the smart Café Royal (part of the Hotel Pucić Palace, *see page 85*) and Kamenica, a popular, long-established place serving great seafood and carafes of house wine at very reasonable prices *(see page 72)*. If you didn't have lunch in the port, this would be a great place for it, or you could return here for an evening meal, when the area is equally lively.

You've reached the end of the itinerary, but if you feel it's time for coffee and cake, go back to Luža Square to the Gradska Kavana or the Café Cele on the corner of Stradun, which does cream cakes. There are conveniently placed post-boxes on the wall if you want to sit here in the shade and write your postcards then pop them straight into a box. If you sit for a while longer, or return here in the evening, you will have a grandstand view of a favoured local activity – strolling, *en famille*, up and down the street, stopping to talk to friends, or having a drink or ice cream at a café table while their invariably well-dressed children play ball, ride bikes or chase each other over the shiny paving stones.

Above: morning market in Gundulić Square

3. AROUND PRIJEKO *(see map, pages 34–35)*

A short walk around the hilly streets north of Stradun, beginning with a visit to the Dominican Monastery. If it coincides with lunchtime, there is no shortage of places in which to eat.

From Luža Square, go through the archway by the Sponza Palace, past stalls offering embroidered cloths and trinkets, and follow Ulica Sv. Dominika for a few metres. To the right, another arch leads out to the Old Port. Straight ahead is a graceful Gothic staircase leading to the monastery. At the top of the steps, on the right, is the **Galerija Sebastian** (open Mon–Sat 9am–7pm; free), where changing exhibitions of modern art are held (and works sold) in the 15th-century votive church of St Sebastian, here the cool, white vaulted rooms make an attractive exhibition space.

The Dominican Monastery

Enter the **Dominikanska Crkva i Samostan** (Dominican Church and Monastery; open 9am–6pm; entrance fee) through a peaceful cloister, where late-Gothic arcades are embellished with Renaissance motifs. In the centre is a huge well that was last used to supply water for the besieged city in 1991–92. Like its Franciscan counterpart, the cloister was used in the 19th century as barracks and stables by both French and Austrian troops.

Among the excellent paintings in the museum are three by Nikola Boži-darević (*c.* 1460–1518): the lovely *Holy Conversation* (1513), showing the Virgin and Child with saints and angels; *The Annunciation*, painted some 10 years later; and *The Virgin with Saints*, in which Mother and Child are flanked by saints Blaise and Paul on one side and Dominic and Augustine on the other. Also look out for Mihajlo Hamzić's tryptych, commissioned by the wealthy Lukarević family in 1512, showing an avuncular St Nicholas framed by a Renaissance-style shell. There are also a number of illustrated manuscripts and a collection of reliquaries, including one of the head of St Stephen, first king of Hungary (997–1038). The church, remodelled in baroque

style after the 1667 earthquake, has an attractive stone pulpit, and some modern works of art. These include Ivo Dulčić's mosaic altarpiece, Djuro Pulitika's *Holy Family*, a bronze *Virgin and Child* by Ivan Meštrović, and eye-catching stained-glass windows that replaced those shattered during the 1991–92 bombardment.

Prijeko

The street directly opposite the door of St Sebastian is **Prijeko**, which runs along to the far end of Stradun. On the right is the Church of the Holy Rosary, on the left the tiny chapel of St Nicholas – both usually closed. Huddled around the church walls is the **Restaurant Rosarij**, the best place to eat in a street full of restaurants. Pop down the third street on the left – Zudioska – to visit the **Sinagoga Musej** (Synagogue and Museum; open Sun–Fri 10am–8pm; entrance fee). The museum contains parchment Torah scrolls, said to have been brought here by Sephardic Jews after their expulsion from Spain in 1492, as well as embroidered Torah Ark covers, and a list of Dubrovnik's Jewish victims of the Holocaust. On the second floor is a synagogue – small, but more than large enough to accommodate the 12 Jewish families that remain in the city.

Back along Prijeko you will be accosted by waiters inviting you to sit and eat at one of the tables beneath umbrellas. **Ragusa II**, the biggest establishment along here, has been going for decades. Look up the steep streets to your right, and climb them if you have the energy. **Kuniceva** is one of the prettiest, with potted plants lining the steps and balconies bright with flowers.

Images of War

Two streets along from Kuniceva, in Antuninska (on the left) you will come to the cosy Talir bar, its walls covered with photos of its arty customers, and some original paintings, more of which can be seen in the tiny gallery of the same name opposite. A few doors further down is **War Photo Limited** (open daily 9am–9pm, summer only; entrance fee), an innovative gallery that displays exhibitions of work by award-winning photographers. Exhibitions in 2009 include one on Columbia and another on US service personnel in Iraq. Gallery owner Frederic Hancez, a Belgian businessman, and director Wade Goddard, who first came to the region as a war photographer, aim not to shock or sensationalise, but to show the true face of war and remind us that situations remain unresolved when the world's press moves on.

There are a couple more little streets this side of Stradun to wander up and down before you emerge once more into the town's main artery at the side of the Festival Café, where it is always good to stop for a drink.

Left: *The Annunciation* in the Dominican Monastery Museum
Above: a picturesque street crossing Prijeko

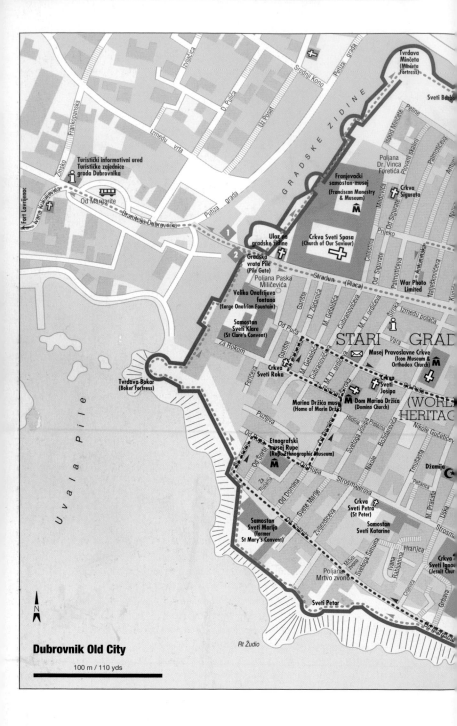

Dubrovnik Old City

100 m / 110 yds

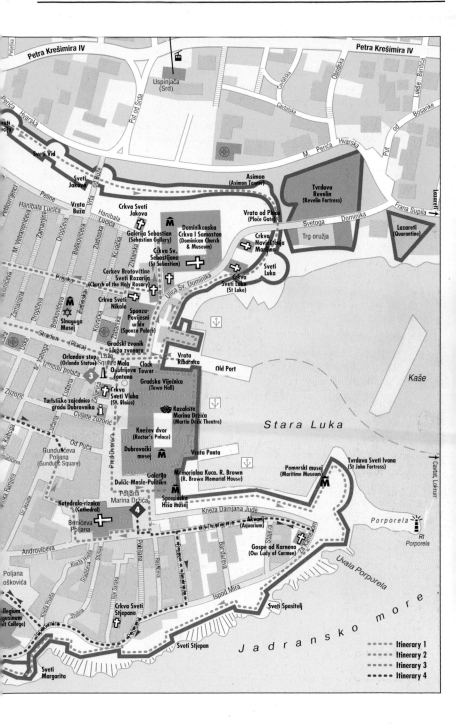

Petra Krešimira IV

Uspinjača
(Srd)

Put od Srđa

Petra Krešimira IV

Obodska

Lukše / Bančica

Cavtatska

M. Perića Hvarska

Put od Bosanke

Perića Hvarska

Sveti Vid

Sveti Jakov

Pelline

Penthionjanci

M. Vetranovićeva

Zamanjina

Hanibala Lucića

Prijeko

Dropčeva

Brsovićeva

Zudiovska

Kovačka

Zlatarska

Asimon
(Asimon Tower)

Vrata od Ploča
(Ploče Gate)

Tvrdava Revelin
(Revelin Fortress)

Frana Supila

Lazareti
(Quarantine)

Vrata Buža

Hanibala Lucića

Crkva Sveti Jakova

Galerija Sebastian
(Sebastian Gallery)

Dominikanska Crkva I Samostan
(Dominican Church & Museum)

Crkva Sv. Sebastijana
(St Sebastian)

Cerkev Brotovčtine Sveti Rozarija
(Church of the Holy Rosary)

Svetoga   Dominika

Trg oružja

Crkva Navješćenia Marina

Sveti Luka

Ulica Sv. Dominika

Crkva Sveti Luke
(St Luke)

Crkva Sveti Nikole

Sponza-Povijesni u liv
(Sponza Palace)

Sinagoga Musej

Zamanjina

Dropčeva

Od Puča

Zuzorić

Garišta

Kovačka

Gradski zvonik i luža zvonara

Stradun (Placa)

Uska

Nr. Kaboga

Orlandov stup
(Orlando Statue)

Vr. između potača

Zeljarica

Luža Square Mala

Turistička zajednica grada Dubrovnika

Crkva Sveti Vlaha
(St. Blaise)

Onofrijeva fontana

Clock Tower

Vrata Ribarnica

Old Port

Kaše

Stara Luka

Kneza Damjana Jude

Gradska Vijećnica
(Town Hall)

Kazalište Marina Držića
(Martin Držić Theatre)

Knežev dvor
(Rector's Palace)

Dubrovački musej

Vrata Ponta

Pomorski musej
(Maritime Museum)

Tvrdava Sveti Ivana
(St John Fortress)

Gundulićeva Poljana
(Gundulić Square)

Od Puča

Ul. Kaboga

Ilije Sarake

Preð Dvorom

Galerija Dulčić-Maslo-Pulitiko

Memorialna Kuca. R. Brown
(R. Brown Memorial House)

Poljana Marina Držića

Spominska Hiša musej

Akvarij
(Aquarium)

Porporela

Rt Porporela

Katedrala-riznica
(Cathedral)

Beničeva Poljana

Androvićeva

Poljana ošković

Podostana

Restićeva

Ul. Pustijerna

Bandureva

Ispod Mira

Gospe od Karmena
(Our Lady of Carmen)

Za Rudiron

Uvala Porporela

Illegium gusinum it College)

Od Kaštela

Crkva Sveti Stjepana

Kneza Iveiša

Gradička I naša

Stulina

Ilije Saraka

Sveti Spasitelj

Sveti Stjepan

Jadransko more

Sveti Margarita

╌ ╌ Itinerary 1
╌ ╌ Itinerary 2
• • • • Itinerary 3
▪ ▪ ▪ Itinerary 4

4. BENEATH THE WALLS: SOUTH OF STRADUN
(see maps, pages 34–35 and 38)

This walk through a quiet area of the Old Town can be done in about two hours, but there are opportunities to extend it by stopping for a swim, or for a drink with a spectacular sea view.

Take swimming kit if you want to drop into the sea to cool off. Otherwise you need nothing but a keen eye and your curiosity.

Start outside the main door of the Cathedral and climb a few steps to the Amoret restaurant *(see page 71)*, where you turn left along Od Pustijerne, a cool, shady street of stone arcades. You could take another left turn where a sign says **Akvarij** (also prominently signed from the Old Port) to visit the small and not very exciting **Aquarium** (open daily 9am–8pm; entrance fee). Otherwise, continue to the end of the street where the church of **Gospe od Karmena** (Our Lady of Carmen) is being renovated and you'll come to a quaint homemade sculpture garden, full of cats, with a sign requesting donations for their care.

The first two narrow streets to the right are blocked off here, restricting entry to an area devastated by the 1979 earthquake, but retrace your steps a short way and go up Braće Andrijića, past crumbling mansions with heraldic crests over the doors. The street was named after the Andrijić brothers, stonemasons from Korčula, and two streets along, in Restičeva, you will see one of their greatest works, the Renaissance Skočibuha Palace, now dilapidated and forlorn. At the top of Braće Andrijića you come to the foot of the city walls, where you turn right into Ispod Mira. A short way along, a gateway in the wall leads down to a concreted bathing area – you will notice it by a sign scrawled on the wall saying 'No Topless, No Nudist', although someone has tried to eradicate the negative. If you feel like a swim, this is your chance. Otherwise, continue beneath the walls. The sounds of students practising at the nearby music school may reach your ears, and you will pass a tiny square where the **Ekvinocijo** restaurant *(see page 72)* offers organically grown produce.

The Jesuit Church

Briefly leave the shadow of the walls when you see, to your right, the great bulk of **Crvka Sveti Ignacija** (Jesuit Church; usually open 8am–6pm; free). Poljana Boškovića, in which it stands, is a slightly untended neighbourhood square with washing hanging outside a few houses and – unlike the church – no pretensions at all. Unless you arrive here when a tour group is visiting, you could be in a village square, although you are only about 200 metres/yards from the centre of town. The church was designed by Jesuit Andrea Pozzo and modelled (inside) on the Gesù Church in Rome. Building work began in 1664, was interrupted by the earthquake three years later, and completed in 1725.

You enter through a door flanked by Corinthian columns, to be faced with a massive interior, dominated by marble side altars. The ceiling of the apse, painted by Spanish-Sicilian Gaetano García, shows Ignatius, founder of the Jesuit Order, ascending to heaven amid fluffy white clouds, while the walls are decorated with scenes from his life, and Pozzo's signature *trompe l'oeil* surrounding them. To the right of the main door is an extremely kitsch Grotto of Lourdes, with a pink-and-white Virgin surrounded by plastic flowers and gazing down on a hopeful pilgrim. At the side of the church is the Jesuit College (Collegium Ragusinum) completed in the 1690s after much controversy. Poet Ivan Gundulić (1589–1638) and mathematician Ruder Bošković (1711–87), among other prominent Ragusans, were educated here. To the right of the church the Jesuit Steps sweep down towards Gundulić Square *(see page 31)*.

Back to the Walls

Back under the walls, a sign proclaims 'Cold Drinks with a Beautiful View' and a short way along, this is exactly what you get. Pop through a hole in the wall to find a little café with tables set on terraces cut into the cliff and stunning sea views (the café is closed if the weather is bad). Carry on along Ulica od Kaštela, and allow yourself to be tempted down any of the little stepped streets to your right, bright with flowery window boxes and flapping washing and with impressive stone balconies and decorated stonework on otherwise humble dwellings. The building you soon pass on the left is the former convent of St Mary, now converted into private apartments. It retains its main portal but the complex otherwise looks a bit run down and neglected.

Left: the impressive bulk of the Jesuit Church
Above: hibiscus clambers over walls in Boškovića Square

Museums and Pizzas

After about 100 metres/yards you can follow the walls no longer and must turn down Na Andriji, which takes a sharp turn to the right and deposits you outside the **Etnografski Musej Rupe** (Rupe Ethnographic Museum; open 9am–6pm; entrance fee). This 16th-century building was the store house for the government grain reserves, which were kept in the huge dry wells you can still see in the floors (*rupe* actually means hole or cavern). Upstairs, the museum displays agricultural implements, fishing paraphernalia and ornate festival costumes, but there is a sad lack of information about any of it. The building itself, and the views from the upper windows, are of most interest.

A few metres right of the museum (note the wooden ramps over the steps to enable delivery carts to get up here) take the first left, Od Domino, down past the Domino restaurant and Domino church. The latter is usually closed during the day but is the venue for concerts on Sunday evening *(see page 78)*. Next door is **Dom Marina Držića** (Home of Marin Držić; open Tues–Sun 10am–6pm; entrance fee). Držić (1508–67) is one of Dubrovnik's most revered playwrights, and his works take pride of place in the Summer Festival, but the museum, with a video about his time in Sicna, and a rather quirky (free) audioguide does not give a great deal of insight.

From the museum, go left along Za Rokum – where **Mea Culpa** sells excellent pizzas – and turn right by a small church to reach Od Puča. Historically the street of the silversmiths, busy little Od Puča still has many shops selling gold and silver filigree jewellery, along with souvenir shops, a couple of little galleries, an old-fashioned barber's and a speciality tea and coffee house. On the left is the plain and partially restored **Orthodox Church** (variable hours) and, next door but one, the **Musej Pravoslavne**

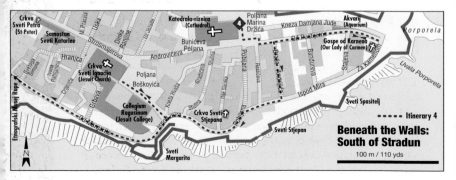

Crkve (Icon Museum; open Tues–Fri 9am–2pm; entrance fee). There is an interesting collection here, from the 15th–19th centuries, but it is easy to miss it altogether, as the entrance is just inside that of Dardin, an upmarket jewellery shop. If you continue along the street a little further you will find yourself in Gundulić Square, or take any turning on the left and you will be back in Stradun.

5. Outside the Ploče Gate *(see map, page 40)*

This walk from Ploče Gate leads northeast along a quiet coast road, visiting the Museum of Modern Art and ending at a secluded cove, with an optional trip to Mount Srd.

The walk, with a visit to the museum, can easily be done in two hours, but if you stop for a swim and a drink at one of the beaches it could make a satisfying half-day out. If you choose to go up to the museum on Mount Srd it will, of course, take longer.

Ploče Gate, like Pile, has a drawbridge and outer and inner gates flanked, morning and evening, by stoical costumed guards and presided over by St Blaise. On the harbour side is the Revelin Club – actually a bar – whose terrace tables offer splendid views and are great for a morning coffee or sunset drink. On the other side looms the bulk of the Revelin Fortress (closed to the public), built to protect the town against Turkish attacks from the interior.

Out on the main road, Frana Supila, the palatial building on your left is a school, as the sounds emanating from inside will tell you. To the right are the walls of the **Lazareti**, the old quarantine hospital, now used mainly as a venue for folklore performances by the Lindo troupe (*see page 78*), and home to a late-night club with appearances by live bands and top DJs. There are a couple of small galleries at street level, and the cavernous rooms below house textile workshops.

Beside a small post office steps lead down to Banje beach, from which you can water-ski. There is another flight of steps further up, near the Excelsior Hotel. Security guards are on duty at either end, but this is a public beach, although the swish Eastwest Beach Club (*see page 77*) has a cordoned-off section where they rent canopied loungers, resembling four-poster beds.

Above left: a café clinging to the walls
Above: heading towards Ploče Gate

Museum of Modern Art

Past the beach, on the left-hand side at No. 23, is the **Umjetnička Galerija** (Museum of Modern Art; Tues–Sun 10am–8pm; entrance fee). It is housed in a beautiful building that looks pure Renaissance but was actually built in 1935 for a wealthy ship owner. When the doors are closed, it is easy to miss the gallery, as its name is displayed only on a discreet plaque to the left of the entrance. The collection, housed over four floors, with sculpture in the courtyard, is rotated, but invariably includes works by Vlaho Bukovac (1855–1922), who, in 1878, was the first Croatian to be accepted by the Paris Salon. Bukovac was born in Cavtat where more of his work can be seen *(see Excursion 3)*.

Upstairs the collection moves further into the 20th century, and includes works by some of the country's best-known modern sculptors, Ivan Kožarić, Frano Kršnić and Ivan Meštrović. There are also paintings by Ivo Dulčić and Duro Pulitika, although many of these are now shown in the gallery opposite the Cathedral *(see page 30)*. On the third floor the palatial salon and terrace threaten to outshine the exhibits; and the top floor is used for changing exhibitions.

Folly and Philosophy

Almost opposite the gallery is the swanky Hotel Excelsior, then the interlinked Villa Orsula and Grand Villa Argentina *(see pages 85–86)*, where the road divides. Take the lower path, Ul. Vlaha Bukovca, where, in lush gardens, stands an Oriental folly, known as the Villa Scheherazade, built in the early 20th century for a wealthy banking family. All you see from the road, peering through Mozarabic wrought-iron gates, is the shiny tiled dome, but you get an excellent view of the folly from the sea on a boat trip to Lokrum *(see page 44)*. Privately owned for many years, the Scheherazade has now been acquired by the Villa Argentina hotel group and will shortly open for business.

Next door, but within the gardens, is a tiny chapel with a bell wall and a plaque on the wall informing passers-by that the mathematician and natural philosopher Marin Getaldić (1568–1626) used to conduct experiments in a cave below (you can see the cave from the sea or when looking back at the end of this walk). Local people were extremely wary of Getaldić, convinced that his activities in the cave must have had something to do with witchcraft.

Walking along this narrow road, with cypresses and century plants growing on the seaward side and oleanders in gardens on the left, you feel as if you are in a country lane. There's litttle traffic, particularly after you pass the newly rebuilt Villa Dubrovnik Hotel. It was unfinished at the time of writing, but despite its incomparable setting it will not be the much-loved hotel of old. A short way along you reach the square-towered former monastery

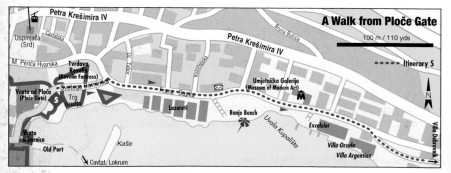

of Sv Jakov (St Jacob), now a private residence, except for the church, which is open only for mass on Sunday at 6pm. Follow the path as it winds down behind the monastery. There are great views back to town (and to Getaldić's cave) and an unmarked flight of steps down to a lovely sheltered beach where there is a snack bar in summer and pedaloes and jet skis for hire.

Nostalgic Corner

Ahead of you is an old, wrought-iron gate on which can just be discerned the words 'Hotel Belvedere'. Through here, to the left, are the derelict remains of the hotel that suffered so badly in the bombardment of 1991–92. So close to the ridge from which shells and artillery were fired, it stood little chance. The upper part of the hotel (accessible from the main road above) has been partially renovated and may one day reopen as a stylish place to stay, but its fate has not yet been decided and sufficient finance has not been forthcoming. At present, it's an eerie, atmospheric spot, especially out of season.

The Imperial Fort on Mount Srd

High on the ridge above Dubrovnik a new **Museum of the Homeland War** has been established in the remains of a Napoleonic fort. Already open although incomplete, it is a moving testimony to the suffering and destruction inflicted on the city. At present access is via a narrow road by private transport or taxi but plans to extend the bus service and rebuild the cable car (destroyed in the war) are underway. The views from the top of the hill are stunning.

Above: Banje beach just outside Ploče Gate

6. LAPAD, BABIN KUK AND GRUŽ *(see map, below)*

Most of Dubrovnik's hotels are to be found on the Lapad and Babin Kuk peninsulas, just a short bus ride from the Old City, and close to Gruž harbour. Although many new developments are changing the face of these suburbs, they remain pleasant, family-friendly tree-filled areas with delightful bays. This route will introduce the area and encompass a two-hour walk around the Babin Kuk headland.

Although many visitors will be based on the peninsulas, for simplicity's sake our route starts with a 10-minute journey on the No 6 bus from the Pile Gate.

The bus route runs west from the Pile Gate past the urban bus station and along the southwest side of Gruž harbour, passing the Hotel Lapad and some magnificent mansions sitting in palm-shaded gardens, to the Orsan Yacht Club. Here it turns away from the harbour and goes uphill, along **Štalište Kralja Zvonimira**. Get off at the post office (ask for the *posta*), cross the main road and walk down the attractive, pedestrianised section of Zvonimira towards the sea. You will pass a number of small hotels (including the recommended Zagreb, *see page 87*) and a whole line of cafés with comfortable swing seats set out on the tiled pavement. Near the end of the street, a little promenade leads off to the left, parallel to the beach (it later becomes Masarykov put, a road lined with big hotels that wends its way up to the headland). On the corner is the **Internet Park**, with tables and computer screens set out under the trees, a children's playground and 'Jumping Park' with bouncy castles, and a row of little kiosks selling tickets for boat trips to the islands *(see page 91)*.

Where Zvonimira meets **Uvala Lapad** (Lapad Bay, shown as Uvala Sumratin on some maps) you will see the big, brash Hotel Kompas, the Casa Café and the beginning of a narrow path that leads westwards along the coast. This is the start of a pleasant walk around the Babin Kuk peninsula, with

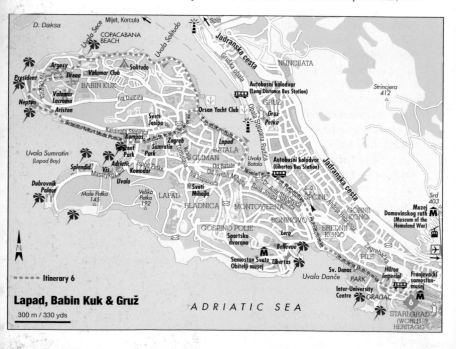

Lapad, Babin Kuk & Gruž

··•··•·· Itinerary 6

300 m / 330 yds

pine trees framing crystal-clear waters, oleanders drooping from gardens, cats dozing in the sun, and plenty of opportunities to swim from the rocks, where ladders have been conveniently placed to help you in and out. At the **Levanat** restaurant *(see page 75)*, where you might like to book for dinner later, the path turns a corner, runs beside the lovely Villa Elita and continues along the coast to the Hotel Neptun, where the terrace makes an ideal spot for a drink, especially at sunset. Go round behind the hotel, turn right and then left at the orange Libertas bus sign. You have to make this small detour to avoid the Dubrovnik President/ Valamar hotel complex *(see page 88)*, which has colonised the tip of the peninsula.

Now go through a small, family-oriented park, with children's play equipment, table tennis, and benches and stone tables. At the other side, bypass a small shopping centre and the Club Exodus and follow the path marked 'Plaža/Beach' a short way down to a little beach known as **Copacabana**, where there is a sports club, a water chute, pedaloes for hire and a café run from a disused chapel. You could stop for a swim or a drink here before following the narrow path marked 'Solitudo' through holm oaks and olive trees, with a view of Daksa island off to the left and the Tudjman Bridge ahead, spanning the estuary. Past a scruffy fishing harbour and the Villa Solitudo (from where you can make diving trips) you come to a line of fishing jetties, and soon are obliged to turn a short way inland and walk between villas and gardens, before emerging at the **Orsan Yacht Club** *(see page 74)*. If it's time for lunch, this is a pleasant place to eat while you watch the yachties loading up. Afterwards, you can either take a sharp right up Zvonimira and back to Lapad Bay, or continue along the side of the harbour, back towards the bus station.

Gruž

Gruž, across the water, does not have a lot to offer the visitor except for lively fruit, vegetable and fish markets (Mon–Sat am), but it is the place to catch the scheduled catamaran to Mljet and the Jadrolinija ferries to Mljet and Korčula and onwards to Split and Bari *(see page 81)*. The long-distance bus station (Autobusni Kolodvor) is a short way from the harbour. If you have time, though, it is worth a wander, especially in the morning when it bustles with local life and gives a very different impression of Dubrovnik from the one you will get in the Old City.

Above: the innovative Internet Park in Lapad
Right: cheerful seaside sculpture

7. LOKRUM ISLAND *(see map, pages 48–49)*

Lokrum lies just a short way from Dubrovnik's Old Port and boats make the 15-minute journey every hour in summer, from 9am; some boats to Cavtat also stop off at Lokrum. It can make a leisurely day trip, if you take a picnic or opt to eat in the restaurant, but it can be seen easily in a couple of hours.

If you want to picnic, buy ingredients in the market in Gundulić Square (see page 31) before you set off. Take swimming things, sunblock and sensible shoes, and don't forget to check the time of the last boat back – currently 6pm.

Lokrum is a peaceful, undeveloped little island. It is scarcely 2km (1 mile) long, and most things of interest to visitors are within 500 metres/yards of the harbour, while the fort on a hilltop can be reached in under half an hour. When you arrive at the jetty, there's a map of the island (but none on sale) and a desk where a small entry charge is made, although this is waived for passengers from the regular ferry service.

Legends of Lokrum

Legend has it that Richard the Lionheart was shipwrecked here on his way back from the crusades at the end of the 12th century and, in gratitude for his survival, built a votive chapel on the island and financed the construction of Dubrovnik's Cathedral. There is no real evidence for this story, but there may be a grain of truth in it somewhere. Another legend tells of a curse placed on Lokrum by Benedictine monks in 1808, after the French governor, put in charge by Napoleon when he dissolved the Ragusan Republic, closed the monastery that had been established there in the 11th century. French rule over Dubrovnik did not last long, and when authority passed to the Austro-Hungarian Empire, it seems the curse went with it. Maximilian, brother of Emperor Franz Josef, bought the island in 1859, converted the monastery and established a botanical garden, which is still there today. Some five years later, however, Maximilian was sent off to Mexico as emperor, a position he held only until 1867, when he was assassinated. Next in line for the curse was Crown Prince Rudolf, son of Franz Josef, who took over the island a dozen years later, but committed suicide in 1889. The lure of Lokrum remained strong, however, and in 1914 Archduke Franz Ferdinand and his wife Sophie planned to spend the summer there. Unfortunately, they went first to Sarajevo, where they were assassinated, and the world was plunged into war.

Top: boats moored off Lokrum. **Above:** Lokrum building in need of some loving care
Right: a view across the rooftops of Dubrovnik to Lokrum Island

Enjoying the Island

Today, Lokrum seems more blessed than cursed. Walk the short distance to the remains of the **monastery**, where there's a friendly, family-run restaurant in the cloister, and fig trees cling to the crumbling walls. Be careful if you have children with you: a huge cistern just outside the cloister is inadequately fenced off. Off to the right (signed from the pathway) is the atmospheric **Botanical Garden**, somewhat run down and overgrown but lush and lovely, as is most of the island. Descendants of the peacocks introduced by Maximilian strut the paths and squawk from their perches in the trees, totally unconcerned by the presence of humans.

A few hundred metres southeast of the monastery is the **Mrtvo More** (Dead Sea), a shallow saltwater lagoon surrounded by flowery shrubs and filled with clear warm water – ideal for swimming. You can also swim off the rocks here and at several other points around the island. Those who prefer calm waters will opt for the lagoon or the little beach near the harbour, while those in search of solitude or more challenging waves will head for the rocks on the southern side.

If you have the energy you can also climb up to the ruined **fort**, built by the French on a hill to the west of the monastery (also signposted). There's not a great deal left of the structure, but the views are splendid and you will be accompanied on your way by butterflies flitting around you and bird calls from above.

That's all there is to Lokrum, but it's a little haven of tranquillity and a peaceful retreat from the city.

Excursions

1. THE ELAPHITE ISLANDS *(see map, pages 48–49)*

A day trip to three islands lying just north of Dubrovnik. There is not a great deal to do on any of them, but they are peaceful, pretty places, where you can get a glimpse of rural life, and no visit to Dubrovnik is complete without seeing them. The name means Deer Islands, but there are no deer there now, although there are rumours of wild boar on Šipan.

Scheduled ferries run from Gruž harbour to the Elaphites several times a day in summer, but in order to see all three islands it is easier to take one of the excursions that are advertised all over the city. You can opt for one that offers lunch, in a Lopud restaurant or a so-called 'fish picnic' on board, or you can be independent and spend your time on the islands as you wish. If you are in Dubrovnik for an extended stay you could always decide to return later by ferry to the island you liked best (see page 91 for more details of excursions and ferries).

Most boat trips start from the harbour at Lapad, from where it is approximately 40 minutes to Koločep, the first and smallest of the islands. Look back to land and you will see, above the mouth of the estuary, the striking new Tudjman Bridge (named after independent Croatia's first president Franjo Tudjman, who died in 1999), carrying traffic towards Split and Zagreb. As you travel up the coast you will notice how bleak the hillsides are, yellow with broom in early summer but otherwise quite bare, which makes the wooded islands, when you reach them, all the more attractive. A short way out to sea you pass Daksa, which belongs to the Elaphite chain but is uninhabited and said to be up for sale.

Koločep

On reaching **Koločep**, boats dock at **Donje Čelo**, a pretty little harbour with a narrow strip of sandy beach, a modern hotel with a pool (Villa Koločep, tel: 021-757 025), a few cafés and, at the far end, the Villa Ruža Restaurant, in an old stone building, with tables set out beneath pine trees. If you come here under your own steam, you could take the wooded paths across the island to the other little settlement, **Gornje Čelo**, but an excursion will not leave you time to do more than walk the length of the harbour, pop into the souvenir shop, and have a dip in the sea and a coffee in one of the cafés by the jetty.

Left: donkeys are still used to carry heavy loads
Right: approaching Lopud on a wooden boat

Šipan

Many boats go next to **Šipan** *(right)*, the furthest island (about 45 minutes), leaving Lopud as the last stop so that passengers have the most time there for lunch, swimming and exploration. Some trips ignore Šipan altogether, but this is a pity; it is worth taking a tour that includes it, even if for only a brief stop. Šipan is the largest island but the least developed for tourism. It is more agricultural than the oth-

ers and its once-flourishing olive groves and oil production are being revived, but the population is low – fewer than 500 – and it is hard to imagine young people staying here once they grow up. Both scheduled ferries and excursion boats stop at **Sudurad**, to the southeast, a tiny harbour where houses shelter beneath vines, olives are cultivated on small terraces and gardens are bright with flowers. A little snack bar at the end of the harbour holds a huge olive press and grinding wheel and has an inviting open hearth that keeps the family warm in winter, although the restaurant, like the rest of the port's establishments, is only open in the summer months.

Two sturdy towers looming up above the harbour belong to the 16th-century summer residence of wealthy shipowner Vice Stjepović-Skočibuha. Approach it from the steps on the other side and you will be able to see down into its cultivated gardens. The residence has been renovated and

Elaphite Islands and the Coast

8 km / 5 miles

now serves as a conference centre but also has a café and restaurant open to the public (tel: 021-758 046, www.sipanmarusic.com). If you have time (you won't if you are on a 'three islands trip') you could walk to **Šipanska Luka**, the island's other port, about 5km (3 miles) to the northwest, dawdling past olive groves and small vineyards edged with drystone walls.

Lopud

Lopud is the final stop, about 15 minutes later. During the Ragusan Republic this was a thriving port, with a population more than 10 times that of today – which is around 300. It produced several Admirals of the Fleet and was the birthplace of Miho Pracat (1528–1607) who, after coming close to financial ruin following two disastrous voyages, finally made a fortune, which he left to the Republic when he died without an heir *(see Route 2)*. There is just one settlement on Lopud now – the little port of the same name – but it is increasingly attracting visitors who make it their holiday base, staying in one of the two hotels *(see below)* or in the private rooms and apartments you will see on offer. If you enjoy tranquillity, it is a perfect place to stay, only 55 minutes from Dubrovnik via the direct ferry, and the last ferry in summer runs from the city late in the evening. However, if you were unlucky enough to experience a spell of bad weather, you could feel pretty isolated here.

Disembarking from the ferry, get your bearings by turning left above the port, past the post office and the elegant Hotel Villa Vilina *(see page 89)* to visit the church of **St Mary of Spilica** (Gospa od Spilica). It is attached to a Franciscan monastery established here in 1483, which served as a place of refuge for the islanders as well as performing a religious function. The church has some beautiful paintings and 15th-century carved choir stalls, but is suffering badly from damp and is undergoing renovation. The cloisters, which are lovely, are also being restored and are not accessible to the public at present.

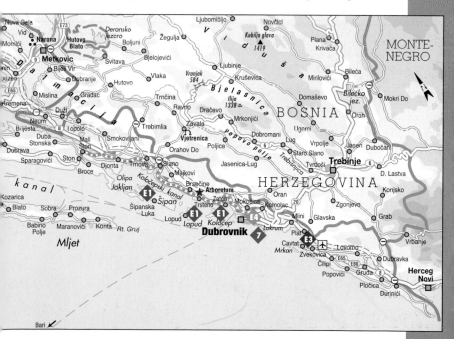

A Harbour Walk

Back at the jetty there is a small museum and treasury on the other side of the road, but they are usually closed. Walk the length of the oleander-lined harbour towards, at the far end, the modern Hotel Lafodia (tel: 020-759 022, www.lafodiahotel.com), which has a pool, its own jetty, and perfect views. En route you will see, beside an imposing but usually closed church, a sign saying Grand Hotel. Venture up the palm-shaded drive through the overgrown gardens and you will find a concrete, modernist building, constructed in 1936, as a sign on the wall informs you, but now deserted and forlorn. There are plans to renovate and re-open the hotel, but funds do not seem to be forth-coming at present. Close by are two tiny chapels, one dedicated to St Jerome, who was born in Dalmatia; the other, the Chapel of the Holy Cross, belonged to Miho Pracat (whose statue is in the atrium of the Rector's Palace in Dubrovnik), and his home is believed to have been next door. All that stands there now is a derelict cottage

Unless you opt to go a short distance up the hill opposite the jetty to eat at the recommended **Terrasse Peggy**, you could choose to have lunch in one of the pleasant harbourside restaurants, with tables by the water's edge (the **Obala**, at No 18, is a good choice for fresh fish and chilled rosé wine from Hvar, *see page 75*).

Across the Island

Afterwards, take the path marked **Plaža Sunj** beside the Grand Hotel and follow it for about half an hour through pine-scented woods, with conve-niently situated benches, to the lovely, sandy **Sunj Bay**. The water is shal-low and safe for children, there are a couple of summer cafés, toilets and showers, and loungers and parasols for hire. But don't imagine that it's going to be a secluded spot just because it was a bit of a hike to get here. All excursion boat passengers will have been advised that it's the best beach on the island, and one of the few sandy ones in this rocky region – some-thing that local people know well. Those who are staying on Lopud have the pleasure of knowing that when the last boat departs for Dubrovnik the beach will be all theirs.

2. MLJET *(see map, page 52)*

Mljet (pronounced *Mlyet*) is a beautiful island to the northwest of Dubrovnik. It makes a delightful day out from the city, but there is accommodation if you want to stay longer.

The catamaran Nona Ana *leaves Gruž harbour at 9am every day in summer (tickets on the boat or from the kiosk over the road, by the Jadrolinija ferry office, 120 kn return). Make sure you get off at the second port, Polače, about 1¼ hours' journey away, not at Sobra on the eastern end of the island, which has little of interest. The return boat leaves Polače at 6.20pm. Take swimming gear, and a picnic if you don't want to eat at one of the restaurants. Several agencies run excursions to Mljet for an all-in price, with a guide, and you may prefer to do it that way, but getting there under your own steam is not difficult.*

Unlike the bare mainland coastline you will have got used to since the boat left Dubrovnik, Mljet is richly forested and delightfully shady. It covers roughly 100 sq km (38 sq miles) and the western end, where the catamaran will dock, is a National Park, established in 1960, whose area of 31 sq km (12 sq miles) encompasses several small settlements, the port of Pomena, and the hotels and restaurants within them, as well as the lakes and surrounding terrain. You can hire a bike directly opposite the jetty, or a beach buggy or scooter from Mini Brum 100 metres/yards or so to the left, but most people head for the National Park kiosk just to the right. Here you pay your entrance fee (90 kn), which includes mini-bus transport to and from the park, and the boat fare out to Sveta Marija (St Mary's Island). The fee may seem a bit steep, and it has increased quite sharply, but all the profits are ploughed back into the upkeep of the park. (Incidentally, if you make your own way to the park entrance you still pay the same amount.)

Previous page: sleepy little Sudarad harbour on Šipan Island
Left: boats are the only way to get around. **Above:** Veliko Jezero, Mljet

St Mary's Island

A five-minute bus ride takes you to **Pristanište** on the shore of **Veliko Jezero** (Big Lake), actually a tidal expanse of saltwater, fed by the sea. Here you can board a small boat (at 10 minutes past each hour) that will take you out to the island of **Sveta Marija** (St Mary). The Benedictine monastery and church here have a chequered architectural history. The church and parts of the monastery are Romanesque, and date from the 12th century, but there were 14th-century additions and a lot of changes in the subsequent two centuries, when it was given a Renaissance façade. After the monks abandoned the place in 1808 it fell into disrepair and is now being renovated by the St Mary's Foundation, in conjunction with the Diocese of Dubrovnik, to which it was handed back in 1997 under the Law of Returned Property. The church, an imposing

single-naved structure, is coming along nicely and can be visited but the monastery and cloister are still under wraps and closed to visitors. However, the ground floor functions as the **Restaurant Melita** (there was a hotel of the same name here in the communist era), and it's a lovely place for an early lunch, right on the water's edge. Try the pancakes made with eggs fresh from the chickens kept in a run beside the monastery vegetable garden.

Before you eat, however, wander along the shady island paths, which won't take more than about 15 minutes, even if you stop to visit the two little votive

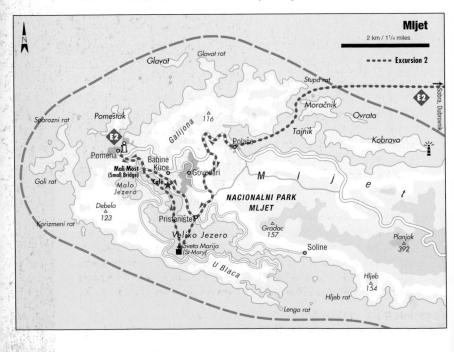

chapels, built by grateful sailors who had survived watery misfortunes. If it's too early for lunch, have a cool drink and an ice cream, take a dip off the rocks then dry out in the sun before getting the boat back to shore (45 minutes past each hour). The trip will not go directly to your starting point, but will take you to **Mali Most** (Small Bridge) on the edge of **Malo Jezero** (Small Lake). Here there's a small swimming beach and opportunities to rent kayaks, canoes and rowing boats, popular activities for those who want to be on the water rather than in it.

A path, marked 'Pomena' – all the park's paths are clearly signposted – takes you round the side of the Small Lake along on a pleasant route, easy underfoot, bordered by pines and olive trees, and with bright yellow butterflies fluttering along ahead of you. After a while the path leaves the lake and goes up a fairly gentle wooded hill, then descends to the little settlement of **Pomena**. Once a tiny fishing village, it is now Mljet's tourist centre – but a restrained and pretty one. The **Hotel Odisej** (tel: 020-362 111, fax: 020-744 042, www.hotel odisej.hr) dominates the bay. The name (Odyssey) relates to the popular myth that Ulysses stopped on Mljet during his voyage. Like all the best myths this one is completely unsubstantiated, but he might well have stopped here if he'd known how lovely it was. Some smart yachts bob in the little bay, and there are several modest restaurants, as well as the one attached to the hotel.

Follow a newly made path round to the right of the harbour to find a row of little eating places. One, the **Galija**, also offers simple, inexpensive rooms (no breakfast; tel: 020-744 029) and has lobsters in a brick tank on the terrace, so visitors can choose which one they want for lunch. Lobster is advertised at many restaurants on the island but, as everywhere else, it is expensive, usually priced by the kilo, at around 450 kn. There's plenty of other seafood though, at good prices, and Pomena would make a delightful lunch stop if you didn't eat on the island. There are more opportunities to rent buggies here from Mini Brum, many of them painted to resemble tigers, zebras or monkeys, and bikes can be hired from the hotel.

Back to the Boat

When you are ready to head back the 2.5 km (1.5 miles) to Pristanište to pick up the minibus, retrace your steps as far as Mali Most and continue along the lake shore. You will pass a pretty settlement, **Babine Kuce**, where there is another opportunity to eat or drink at Mali Raj, on a geranium clad terrace beneath a vine. Don't linger too long, as there's only one boat back. If you have time and can't resist the lure of the lakes, you can pass the pick-up point and clamber down to the water's edge for another swim. As long as there are no signs prohibiting swimming, and you are not near the seaward exit from the lake, where the current is strong, you may swim anywhere.

Back in Polače, you could wander around the ruined walls of a Roman palace to the right of the National Park kiosk, but this won't detain you for

Above left: St Mary's Monastery, Mljet
Right: oleanders bloom all over the island

long. Better to sit in one of the cafés that line the waterfront, enjoy the smell of woodsmoke as restaurateurs fire up their barbecues, and sample the local dessert wine, *prošek*, while you wait for boarding time.

This route has been designed for those who only have a day to spare. If you have longer, there is a wealth of trails to explore in the park, none of them too taxing, although there are a few steep gradients. For 3 kn you can buy a map with marked trails from one of the official kiosks. And, if you have transport, you could follow the road through the centre of the island and drop down to the south coast to visit Ulysses Cave – one of many along the limestone karst coast, although this one is said to have sheltered Ulysses. If you plan to stay for more than a day, you could check www.croatia-mljet-apartment. com for accommodation. If you just get so carried away with the island that you miss the boat back to Dubrovnik, you will have to knock on one of the doors advertising *sobes* – rooms for rent.

3. CAVTAT *(see map, page 56)*

Cavtat is a pretty village about 17 km (10 miles) south of Dubrovnik, on a peninsula between two bays. It was the site of the Roman settlement of Epidaurus and the place from which the Illyrian inhabitants fled in the 7th century to found Ragusa. The foundations of a fort on the tip of the peninsula are all that remain of the Roman period. The activities in this route, including a leisurely lunch, could be accomplished in about five hours.

In summer, boats leave the Old Harbour for Cavtat throughout the day. The regular service takes about 45 minutes, but some boats stop at points along the coast and take longer – check when you book. Fast Nova Expressway boats do the trip in 30 minutes. The last boat back from Cavtat is usually about 5.30pm, but the Nova boats run later. There are also buses, a good choice if the sea is rough.

Above: lobster fisherman on Mljet. **Above right**: Račić Family Mausoleum
Right: Cavtat harbour and the monastery church

excursions

A visit to **Cavtat** (pronounced *Tsaftat*) is one of the most popular day trips from the city. As your boat approaches the harbour, you will have a picture-postcard view of a palm-lined promenade with a church at either end, and inviting-looking restaurants and cafés in between. To the right, as you disembark, is the parish church of **Sveti Nikole** (St Nicholas) and, signposted on the road to the left, the Pinoteka (Gallery of St Nicholas; open 10am–1pm; entrance fee). Beside the church the **Rector's Palace** contains a gallery (currently closed, tel: 020-478 556) housing the library and paintings, costumes and other items collected by Vlaho Bogišič, a writer and lawyer born here in 1834, whose bulky statue sits opposite. Beside him is a triangle of restaurants, of which the best known is **Leut** *(see page 76)*, run by the same family since 1971.

Monastery and Mausoleum

Going back along the harbour front, picking your way between restaurant tables, and passing the attractive little **Hotel Supetar** *(see page 89)*, you reach the **Franjevački Samostan Crkva**
(Franciscan Monastery Church; usually open; free). The eye-catching polyptych of St Michael (1510) to the left of the door is the work of Vicko Dobrečević, son of Lovro *(see Route 1)*. One oddity in this plain and peaceful little church (although it is not uncommon in Croatia) is a dis-embodied hand appearing from the pulpit, holding a crucifix.

Behind the church, turn left into Ul. Katernikova (where the Hotel Villa Kvaternik is located, *see page 89*), then continue up a flight of steps to the hilltop cemetery, dominated by the **Mausolej Obiteliji Račić** (Račić Family Mausoleum). This octagonal, white marble structure was designed in 1922 by Ivan Meštrović, the best-known 20th-century Croatian sculptor, for the super-wealthy shipowning family. Its bronze doors, with images of four Slav saints, are guarded by a

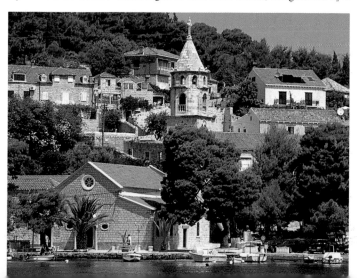

pair of Art Nouveau-style angels, while another angel flexes his wings on the cupola. The Račićs, who followed each other to the mausoleum in quick succession in the 1920s, obviously wanted to appear as opulent in death as they were in life.

Around the Peninsula

After admiring the sweeping views up and down the coast, leave the cemetery by the back gate and follow a sloping path through pine woods. Where the path divides, you could take the right fork and follow it around the outside of town, to arrive back at the church of St Nicholas. Better, though, to take the steps down to a bathing area, where there's a beach café, and a concreted path continues along the waterside to Cavtat's second bay, **Uvala Tiha**; here, coaches and public buses wait, and the bay-side Konoba Ivan (opposite) serves good food at reasonable prices.

The road parallel to the bay, past the police station and a small branch of the tourist office, soon becomes quieter, more rural, lined with cypresses, then widens out again when it reaches the Hotel Albatross, looking a bit like a terracotta cruise ship built around a swimming pool. A short distance further along, at the Hotel Epidaurus, the path peters out altogether.

A Detour

Those with more time, strong shoes and plenty of energy may like to try the **Ronald Brown Trail**, which starts behind the Albatross and leads to a cross on a hilltop, marking the spot where the plane carrying the US Secretary of Commerce and the rest of a trade delegation to Croatia crashed in 1996. There is a small memorial room dedicated to Brown in Dubrovnik (*see page 30*), and conspiracy theories about the crash abound on the internet. The trail takes about two hours, winding steeply uphill.

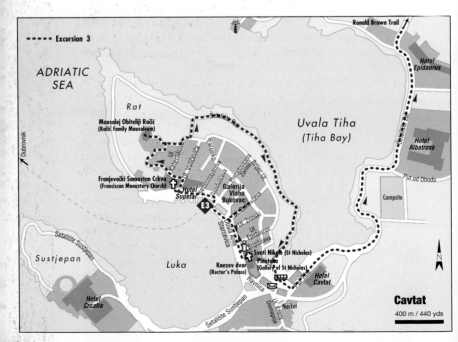

Bukovac's Gallery

Now return to the harbour for lunch, if you haven't already done so, and after you've sat in the sun for a while to aid your digestion, it will be time to move on. Take the fifth little lane on your right from the promenade, Ul. Bukovčeva, to visit the **Galerija Vlaho Bukovac** (open Tues–Sat 9am–1pm, 4–8pm, Sun 4–8pm; entrance fee), dedicated to Bukovac (1855–1922), the highly esteemed and prolific artist who was born here *(see Route 5)*. Bukovac had a hard life as a young man, but was accepted by the Paris École des Beaux Arts after gaining the financial backing of the enlightened Bishop Strossmeyer. The artist worked for many years in Zagreb before becoming a professor at the Prague Academy.

The ground floor of the house is empty except for some modern paintings, but the walls and staircases throughout are colour-washed and decorated with friezes depicting birds, animals and rural scenes – all done by Bukovac. Upstairs, two large rooms display many of his portraits, mostly of family members – detailed, contemplative and extremely memorable. One chilling picture, in a room by itself, apparently shows the heads of the artist and his wife lying on a table, looking up at those of four children, suspended by their hair.

Your visit to the museum over, you will have time for a coffee on the seafront while you watch your boat appearing over the horizon. A word of warning: if the sea gets really choppy while you are here, the smaller boats will not make the journey, so you will have to go back by bus. This is no great hardship: bus No.10 runs regularly from the terminal in Tiha Bay, where a timetable is posted, to Dubrovnik bus station, with stops en route; the journey takes about half an hour, and the fare is currently 12 kn.

Above: a boat trip to Cavtat is on the itinerary of most visitors

4. TRSTENO AND STON *(see map, pages 48–49)*

Trsteno is a tiny village about 18km (11 miles) up the coast from Dubrovnik that has gained a wide reputation for its Arboretum. The twin villages of Ston and Mali Ston on the Pelješac peninsula are known principally for having some of the best oysters in the world and for their huge defensive walls, claimed to be second only to the Great Wall of China.

It would be best to hire a car for this trip, as buses to Ston are infrequent, and you might like to combine it with the next excursion and stay overnight in Korčula (see page 60). If you just want to visit Trsteno, the bus to Split, approximately every hour from the long-distance bus station at Gruž harbour (tel: 060-30 50 70), will drop you off there, and will also stop at Zaton.

If you are driving, follow signs to Split, which take you up above the town and across the impressive Tudjman Bridge. From there it's a pleasant 10-km (6-mile) drive to **Zaton**, which is divided in two: Veliki (Large) and Mali (Small), together forming an attractive little settlement that is building up its tourist infrastructure, catering to those who want to be outside Dubrovnik but within easy reach of the city. There are a number of residences that were once the summer retreats of wealthy families and, signposted from the main road, a good, family-run restaurant – the **Orsan** (tel: 020-891 267), set in an old boathouse, after which it is named.

The Arboretum

Some 8km (5 miles) further on you reach **Trsteno**, where two huge 500-year-old plane trees dominate the main street. Turn left beside the trees down a narrow road and you will shortly reach the **Arboretum** (open summer: daily 8am–7pm; winter 8am–5pm; entrance fee), which now belongs to the Croatian Academy of Science and the Arts. Established as a summer home and garden in the late 15th century by Ivan Gučetić, a prominent member of Ragusa's nobility, it has changed and expanded over the years and now covers an area of 25 hectares (63 acres). The collection includes more than 300 species of trees, shrubs and plants, some rare and exotic, in a delightful setting running down to the sea, which makes

a lovely, shady place to spend some time on a hot summer's day.

Towards the end of 1991, the Arboretum came under a dual attack from sea and air, and much of it was destroyed in the subsequent fire, although the oldest part escaped without too much damage. A great deal of restoration has been done since then, and the garden, a mixture of formal and semi-wild areas, is delightful – as is the over-the-top, 18th-century Neptune's Grotto, with dolphin fountains and water lilies. If you are driving, park in the designated area and you will see nearby a sign pointing towards a little beach to which you can make your way if you feel like a swim after you have explored the garden.

Ston

Follow the coast for another 30km (18 miles) or so and you will come to Ston, which, like Zaton, is divided in two. The larger village is sometimes called **Veliki (Large) Ston**, and the smaller is always known as **Mali (Little) Ston**. They sit at the head of the **Pelješac peninsula**, divided by a narrrow isthmus. The 5km (3 miles) of great walls that connect the two (and for which World Heritage status is being sought) were built in the 14th century, principally to protect the salt pans, which you will see as you drive between the two settlements. Still in use today (you can buy little cloth bags of Ston salt, which make a nice souvenir) they were once vital to Ragusa's economy and were much coveted by Napoleon. The energetic can climb the walls from Veliki Ston for fabulous views of the salt pans and the surrounding area.

You reach Mali Ston first, but save this for later and turn left instead, and drive about 2km (1 mile) to Ston. The Veliki is a misnomer: although it's called a town, and it has a long history, having been founded in 1333, it is not much more than a village, with a population of scarcely 600. Ston has little to offer in the way of sites or entertainment, but it's an appealing and friendly little place with several churches and a morning market, and the café tables set out in the central square, shaded by lime trees and flowering shrubs, make it a good place to stop for coffee. The area was badly hit by an earthquake in 1996 (fortunately with no loss of life), and there are still some signs of damage, but much of it has been well repaired.

Left: you have to cross the Tudjman Bridge when driving up the coast
Above: walking the great wall at Ston. **Right:** bell wall and tower in Veliki Ston

Shellfish Centre

Return now to Mali Ston, which is tiny, just a cluster of houses around a fortified tower, set beside a bay that gives the place its *raison d'être* – oysters. You will have seen the expanses of oyster beds as you approach the

village. The best-known restaurant, the **Villa Koruna** (which also has accommodation, tel: 020-754 359), displays a certificate awarded at the London International Food Fair in 1939, when the osyters were proclaimed the best in the world. That seems a very long time ago, and many things have changed since then, but the oysters – and the mussels – still rank among the best and bring flocks of people here for Sunday lunch. And lunch is what you will probably be interested in as well. If the Koruna – with its huge tanks of fish and a couple of slowly circling turtles – is busy with tour groups, as it sometimes is, walk round to the left of it, past the great tower. Here you will find the Taverna Bota Šare and the Kapetanovs Kuča, both of which offer excellent seafood at tables right beside the bay. If you don't like oysters, don't worry, there's plenty more to choose from: garlicky mussels, black risotto (made with squid ink) and lobster soup, to mention just a few.

5. KORČULA *(see map, page 62)*

The final excursion is to the island of Korčula, which lies 48 nautical miles northwest of Dubrovnik. It is a fertile island, which, like the Pelješac peninsula from which it is separated by a narrow channel, specialises in wine production. The best beaches are on the south of the island, and are worth exploring if you are here on an extended stay, but this excursion concentrates on the walled town of Korčula itself.

You can get to the island by ferry (about 3½ hours) or by faster catamaran if you go on an organised excursion (see page 91). But if you come in winter, or don't fancy such a long boat journey and would like to spend more than a few hours here, you could hire a car, drive the 115 km (70 miles) then make the 15-minute ferry crossing from Orebić, from where boats do operate in winter. You could then spend the night here and perhaps combine the trip with a visit to Ston and Trsteno en route or on the following day (see previous excursion).

Above: people come from miles around to eat shellfish in Ston
Right: St Mark above the cathedral door in Korčula Town

An advantage of driving to Korčula, rather than taking the boat, is the opportunity it offers to admire the landscape of the wooded **Pelješac peninsula** with its pretty roadside shrines, and to stop off at some of the wineries that line the main road; you can usually taste the local produce and buy some if you like it. This area produces some of the best wine in Croatia *(see page 71)* but most of it is for domestic consumption so will be unfamiliar to visitors. The wineries, however, have not been prettied up for tourists: they are clearly no-nonsense working environments.

Getting to the Island

Shortly after the town of Priždrina the vineyards end, the landscape becomes more bare and rocky, and ahead you see the glittering sea, framing the island of **Korčula**. The port of **Orebič**, from where you take the ferry, is small, but there are several hotels and to the north lie some of the coast's best sandy beaches, which are popular with windsurfers. There are car ferries from here, but if you are going to concentrate on the town of Korčula, as this itinerary does, it would be as well to leave your car here and take the passsenger ferry across. The Old Town itself is pedestrianised, and outlying areas are easily reached on foot. As your boat takes you across the narrow chan-

nel, the walled town, with its four sturdy towers, honey-coloured walls and terracotta roofs, resembles a fairy-tale city.

Once in harbour (don't forget to check on return boat times), you will see straight ahead of you a broad flight of steps, dividing around a central fountain. This is **Primorska Vrata** (Sea Gate), one of two entrances to the old town, but before going in you may like to pop into the adjacent tourist office, which is set in a splendid 16th-century loggia. If you are going to stay the night on the island, the elegant **Hotel Korčula** next door is a good choice *(see page 89)*.

The Old Town

At the top of the steps a broad terrace is lined with café tables and straight ahead, a narrow alley (Ul. Dinka Miroševiča) leads up to St Mark's Square where you will find the Cathedral, the Treasury Museum and the Town Museum. The Gothic-Renaissance **Katedrala Sveti Marka** (St Mark's Cathedral; open daylight hours; free) is constructed, like most of Korčula's buildings, from the mellow limestone that made the island, and its stone masters, prosperous and famous. The tower and cupola, dating from

Right: the cathedral square in the heat of the day

around 1480, are the work of Marko Andrjić whose sons, Petar and Josip, worked on numerous prestigious buildings in Dubrovnik, including the Sponza Palace, the Rector's Palace and the Skočibuha Palace *(see Routes 2 and 4)*. Flanking the main doorway are curly-maned lions and some rather lewd naked figures representing Adam and Eve. Above the door sits St Mark, robed as a bishop. Inside, the Cathedral is notable for a splendid, high wooden ceiling; a huge stone canopy, also the work of Andrjić *père*, and built to his own design; and a richly coloured Tintoretto altarpiece (1550) depicting St Mark flanked by St Bartholomew and St Jerome. In the South Aisle there is an *Annunciation* that is ascribed to the School of Tintoretto; and in the North Aisle is Ivan Meštrović's early 20th-century bronze statue of St Blaise.

To the right of the Cathedral is the **Opatska Riznica** (Treasury Museum; open 9am–2pm, 5–8pm; entrance fee). This elegant limestone building houses an eclectic array: its art works range from 15th-century sacred paintings – including a precious polyptych of *Our Lady of Conception* by Blaž Trogiranin, one of the most respected 15th-century Dalmatian artists – to Ivan Meštrović's 20th-century bronze *Pietà*. There are also ecclesiastical robes, chalices and processional crucifixes; and at ground level there's a cool kitchen, with large metal pots in the hearth and shelves stacked with Roman pots and jars of all shapes and sizes, recovered from the sea in the 1960s.

Directly opposite is another museum worth visiting, the **Gradski Muzej** (Town Museum; open Apr–Oct: varied hours; Jul–Aug: 9am–9pm; entrance fee), in a 16th-century Renaissance palace built for the wealthy Gabrielis family. The ground floor has an interesting exhibition on the island's stonemasons; the first floor concentrates on Korčula's second important industry – shipbuilding – which utilised timber from the densely wooded island. At their height, the shipyards rivalled those of Venice and Dubrovnik and at the end of the 18th century there were still 100 shipyards here.

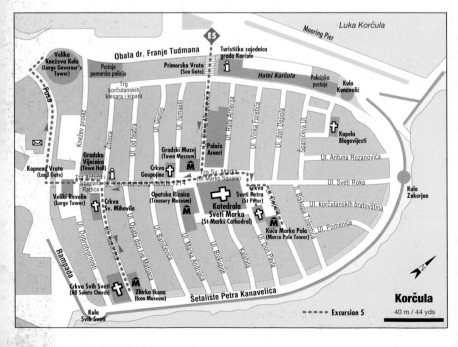

Elsewhere in the museum are rooms housing 17th- to 19th-century furniture, elaborate costumes, portraits of the Andrjić family, kitchen implements and, on the top floor, easily overlooked and not mentioned in the museum's guide, photographs of Tito's Partisans *(see History, page 15)*, including one showing the First Conference of the People's Liberation Council for the district, held in November 1943, along with an ancient typewriter, used by the Partisans.

Time for a Break

If you are hungry, or have had enough of old buildings and museums for the moment, there are plenty of places to sit down and eat. Korčula's restaurants offer the usual selection of seafood and Dalmatian ham, but they specialise in pizzas – and very good ones. Right opposite the Cathedral, you could try the **Pizzeria Caenozzo**, which has good pizzas, salads and sandwiches. The service is friendly, but, due to their location, they do get very busy. For something fishy, go to **Konoba Adio Mare**, a short way down Ul. Sveti Roka, which leads into the square from the left, beside the church of St Peter. They serve tasty grilled squid, among other things, along with local wines. The island's speciality – sea-urchin eggs – may prove more difficult to find, unless you know a local fisherman.

The Marco Polo Experience

It is generally agreed that Marco Polo (1254–1324) was born in Venice, but, as you will soon discover, that is not accepted on this island. Korčula claims the great explorer for its own, believing that he was born here before

Top: Tintoretto altarpiece in Korčula Cathedral
Above: homage to Marco Polo

his family moved to the Italian city of canals. There is a Hotel Marco Polo (on the next peninsula, east of the Old Town), Marco Polo Tours operate close to the harbour, and you can visit the **Kuća Marka Pola** (Marco Polo Tower; open 9am–8pm; entrance fee) in Ul. Depolo, on the right, off Ul. Sveti Roka. However dubious the associations, it's a lovely place, entered through a pretty, vine-covered patio, and with stunning views from the top. The attached building – a graceful, ruined Gothic palace – was purchased by the town council in 2004 and is to be renovated and opened to the public, presumably as Marco Polo's birthplace.

Drop in, next, to the nearby church of **Sveti Petra** (St Peter; open summer: daily 10–7pm; entrance fee), a simple little chapel, and the oldest one in the town, where an exhibition portraying the life of Marco Polo is on display. This is pure kitsch: exhibits include cardboard cut-outs dressed in 13th-century robes, models made of shell and polystyrene depicting pirate ships, and a map on which the explorer's journey flashes in coloured lights. And there's background music.

In late May there is an annual festival called the **Return of Marco Polo**, when a suitably clad character is welcomed by the mayor and led to his home, where he entertains the townspeople with stories of his travels, before they all settle down to a concert of Renaissance music. Korčula is known for its festivals and its desire to keep traditions alive. The most important celebration is the **Moreska**, or Sword Dance Festival, held on St Theodor's Day, 29 July, when lavishly dressed medieval knights perform a stylised dance and play, similar to the Moors and Christians festivals in Spain *(see page 79)*. A shortened version of the dance takes place on an outdoor stage in the Jetno Kino every Thursday in summer (ask the tourist office for details).

Icons and Ice Cream

Leave Marco Polo behind now, and, bypassing the Cathedral, follow the road called Korčulanskog Statuta 1214 (the cumbersome name relates to the City Statute of 1214, one of the oldest Slav legal documents, which laid down the rights and obligations of citizens and regulated trade and agriculture). At the end of the road (only a few hundred metres/yards) turn left into Ul. Kaporova to visit the church of **Svih Svetih** (All Saints; usually open in daylight hours; free) in order to see a beautiful 15th-century

Above: the old kitchen in the Treasury Museum

polyptych by Blaž Trogiranin (whose work is also in the Treasury Museum). Next door is the **Zhirka Ikon**a (Icon Museum; open 10am–2pm; 5–7pm; entrance fee), housed in the Hall of the Brotherhood of All Saints. Painted on wood in tempera and gilt, some of the icons are truly moving.

From here, you could follow the broad, pine-shaded road (Petra Kanavelića) that leads back around the town in an anti-clockwise direction, stopping for an ice cream at one of the cafés. Alternatively, backtrack to the main road, where it opens out into a small square, with the **Gradska Vijećnica** (Town Hall) on the right and, on the left, the 15th-century **Veliklo Revelln** (Large Tower), which guards the **Kopnena Vrata** (Land Gate) to the town.

Outside the Walls

After climbing the tower for far-reaching views of the glistening sea and the coastline, you could go down the steps out of the Old Town and turn right, walking a few metres until you reach the great, cone-shaped **Velika Kneževa Kula** (Large Governor's Tower), built at the western corner of the walls to protect both the Governor's Palace and the harbour. Go left here, and follow the harbour road for a different view of Korčula and the chance for a swim at one of two small bathing beaches. If you want to check out the **Marina**, or are going to stay in one of the hotels on the next little peninsula east, go left when you come out of the Land Gate and follow the road round to the right. Here you'll find opportunities for swimming and sailing (Korčula's a truly great place for sailing and hosts a number of regattas) as well as just sitting by the sea, resting your feet and watching the boats bob in the water.

Above: leave time for a swim after sightseeing
Right: brightly painted boats in the harbour

Leisure Activities

SHOPPING

Dubrovnik is not a place for serious shoppers, or bargain hunters. Prices are similar to those in the rest of Europe for most items, and, while Croatians would love to have access to smart, fashionable clothes and well-designed household goods, the economy is simply not buoyant enough to support many shops selling such things.

If you buy any item that costs more than 500 kuna you are entitled to reclaim VAT (PDV), which is set at 22 percent. When you make your purchase, ask for PDV-P form, which should be completed and stamped on the spot, then verified by the customs service when you leave the country. You then post the verified receipt back to the shop, together with your bank account details. Then you wait for the refund, which will come – eventually. The whole process is so time consuming that it is really only worth doing if you are buying an extremely expensive item.

You will find a range of supermarkets, chemists and tourist kiosks, so there will be no problem finding everyday items that you have forgotten or run out of, from sunblock and shampoo to the 'jelly shoes' that are advisable if you are going to be swimming in rocky areas. The **dm** store, selling cosmetics, toiletries and everything for babies, has set up shop in an elegant building outside the Pile Gate, and in the **docdubrovnik** shopping centre in Lapad. The biggest supermarket is **Tommy**, opposite the bus station. The No 6 bus stops right outside. The Volksbank is on the ground floor, and you take an escalator up to the store. The **Konzum** chain has small branches all over the city, some of them such as the one in **Gunduličeva Poljana** (Gundulić Square), so discreet it is easy to miss them.

Although it is not a shopper's heaven, there are a number of local items that are worth looking out for, including:

Left: time for reflection in the Old Port. **Right:** selling table linen

Embroidery and Lace

You will not have to look far for these items. In fact they are hard to avoid. In the large square just outside Pile Gate, by the bus stops, a number of stalls offer all kinds of embroidered linen and lace, along with handmade dolls and other trinkets. In the Old Port, women sit crocheting and embroidering the goods spread out for sale: tablecloths, napkins, cushion covers, handkerchiefs and baby clothes. More of the same can be found under the archway between Luža Square and the port; and on the steps leading to the Dominican Monastery, where sellers are often dressed in regional costumes The market in Gundulić Square *(see page 69)* is another place to find household linen and lace.

Jewellery

Od Puča, running parallel with Stradun, was the street of the silversmiths, and this is where you will still find lots of little jewellery shops, some of which are old and atmospheric, others stocked with items that may or may not have been made here. Silver filigree is the speciality, and coral also features frequently; prices are reasonable and some of the designs are attractive. A more upmarket jewellery shop is **Galerija Nakita**, accessible from Ulica Miha Pracata 8 and Od Puča (on the ground floor below the Icon Museum). Unusual and striking items are displayed in vaulted rooms and a courtyard, but the staff tend to follow you around in a rather discon-

certing manner. Interesting jewellery can also be found in the **Handmade Jewellery Atelier** at Nalješkovićeva 6, one of the streets leading north from Stradun.

Paintings and Prints

A number of small shops and galleries sell work by contemporary Croatian artists, usually at reasonable prices. You can buy paintings by Đuro Pulitika *(see page 30)*, although these, naturally, will be more expensive. Some of the other work on sale, particularly the Old Town scenes, is in a similar style. There is also a lot of naive art, some of which is quite appealing. In Sv. Dominika (by the Dominican Monastery) you will find interesting works in **Sebastianart** (in the old St Sebastian church) and **Galerija Sv. Luka**. In Marojice Kabog (running between Stradun and Od Puča), the **Atelier Romana Milutin-Fabris** concentrates on the work of this Dubrovnik-born artist. In Lučarica, the next street along, towards St Blaise's Church, the **Artur Galerija** is also worth a look.

Books and Music

The two best bookshops are both in Stradun, on opposite sides of the street: **Algebra** and **Algoritam**. Both have a good selection of books about Dubrovnik, and Croatia in general, and some Croatian phrase books, as well as a small supply of English-language paperback fiction. In addition, Algoritam stocks videos, and CDs featuring traditional Croatian folk music and contemporary pop and rock. Both shops also sell postcards and camera film.

Wine and Food

Vines have been cultivated on Dalmatia's sunny slopes since Roman times. The red wine tends to be robust and full-bodied: Dingač from the Pelješac peninsula and Plavac from Hvar are the most prized. The best-known whites are Grk from the island of Korčula, and Pošip Čara from Hvar. Prošek is a sweet (but not too sweet) dessert wine.

The Croatian national spirit, *rakija*, is made from distilled alcohol flavoured with fruit or herbs. The recipes for it differ not only from place to place but also from distiller to distiller.

A wide range of wines and local spirits can be found in supermarkets – some in attractive bottles, which make nice gifts. For more upmarket choices try **Vinoteka**, a well-stocked wine shop with helpful service on the corner of Od Sigurate and Stradun. **Dubrovačka Kuća** (Dubrovnik House) in Sv. Dominika sells wine, *rakija* and oil, and good-quality but fairly expensive souvenirs. These include embroidered cushion covers and strings of **Licitar hearts**, honey cakes that are dried, painted red and decorated.

Above: colourful hats and bags for sale in the Old Town

They are traditionally used as Christmas decorations or as Valentine's Day gifts. **Bonbonnière Kraž**, on the corner of Zamanjima and Stradun, is a chocolate addict's delight. You can pick-and-mix a variety of sweets and chocolates and buy them by the kilo. Kraž is Croatia's major manufacturer of chocolate and biscuits, and their products can be found in numerous shops, but you won't find such a wide selection elsewhere.

Ties and Hats

Ties, they say, were invented in Croatia. In the mid-17th century the cravat, a loosely tied scarf worn by Croatian soldiers, became popular in Paris when it was seen adorning the necks of Croatian mercenaries in the service of Louis XIII. Charles II introduced the cravat to England, when he returned there from exile in France, and the fashion spread across Europe and later to the Americas.

A range of high-quality pure silk ties, made by the Potomac Company, can be found in **Boutique Croata** at Pred Dvorom 2 (near the Cathedral) and in the same company's outlet in the Hotel Excelsior.

Even if you never wear a hat, **Ronchi**, at Lucarica 2, just off Luža Square, is worth a visit. They have been making hats since 1858 and display some wonderful creations.

Fashion

Although the choice is not extensive, you can find contemporary fashion in Dubrovnik. **Croatia Design** in Zlatarska (between Prijeka and Stradun) has some original and attractive clothes and the prices, while not cheap, are not unreasonable. **JegerStar**, in Od Puča 7, is the most trendy shoe shop, stocking Diesel, Kickers, Nautica and the quirky Camper styles, among others. Diesel is also represented in **Petovrijenci**, just off Stradun. There is a rather refreshing lack of chain stores, but **Dorothy Perkins** has appeared in Stradun and **Benetton** has a branch next to the Gradska Kavana in the Old Town and has recently opened a second one in the **docdubrovnik** shopping centre in Lapad, where you can also find Kookai and OshKosh. The more upmarket **Max Mara** stands opposite the Rector's Palace and **Tommy Hilfiger** has an outlet in Antuninska at the Pile end of Stradun.

Antiques

Izmedju Polača, the street running parallel to Stradun, on the south side, is a good place for antiques. Browse in **Orozel**, at No. 13 where, among the icons, paintings, porcelain, silver and glassware there are some real bargains to be had.

Local Markets

Dubrovnik's markets are the best places to browse and to buy fresh local produce – useful not only for those in self-catering accommodation but for putting together a picnic or simply buying whatever fruit is in season. Early summer is a particularly fruitful time, and you will see (and smell) great pyramids of strawberries piled on stalls alongside ripe peaches, nectarines and apricots. On other stalls, glossy aubergines sit beside piles of chard, spinach, and young courgettes, complete with their yellow flowers.

The main markets are the daily ones in **Gruž Harbour** – where there is also a big, noisy fish market – and in **Gundulićeva Poljana** (Gundulić Square) in the Old Town. The former is a strictly local affair, worth visiting if you can get there early, because this is when Gruž really comes to life – and very convenient if you are about to get on a morning ferry and haven't had time for breakfast.

The Gundulić Square market also specialises in fresh produce but, being in the heart of tourist territory, has goods geared towards foreign visitors as well. You will find embroidered linen and lace, and products derived from locally grown lavender: bottles of oil, attractively wrapped soaps and pretty linen lavender bags, all of which make easy-to-pack souvenirs or gifts to take home. You will also see local honey for sale here, strings of fresh garlic, bags of nuts and little coronets of dried figs, garlanded with leaves.

Visitors staying on the Lapad peninsula could visit the friendly little fresh produce market just off **Štalište Kralja Zvonimira**, the pedestrianised street leading to the sea.

Markets operate only in the morning, every day except Sunday, and all trace of them has usually disappeared by 1pm, leaving only the pigeons pecking at any leftovers they can find.

EATING OUT

Eating out in Dubrovnik is a delight, especially during the summer, when nearly all restaurants have outside tables, either on a terrace, a pavement, or right beside the sea. It does help, however, if you like seafood. Meat does feature *(see below)* but fishy things predominate – as you would expect in a city on the shores of the Adriatic. Anyone familiar with the food served on the coast of Italy, just across the water, will notice many similarities. You will also see a degree of similarity in Dubrovnik's restaurant menus: from the economical to the expensive, they all feature similar dishes, although the standard of cooking and presentation vary a great deal. Menus are invariably translated into English, and often into German and French as well.

Another thing that visitors will notice is that while some establishments are called restaurants, others are known as *konobas*. A *konoba* was originally a kind of taverna, a somewhat humble or rustic place to eat, and in the rural regions this is still the case, but in the city the two words are interchangeable. You may find a relatively expensive restaurant calling itself a *konoba,* while a more basic one is known as a restaurant.

Local Specialities

Prevalent on Dubrovnik's menus is shellfish *(školjke)*, including mussels, which rather confusingly are known both as *mušule* and *dagnje*, shrimps *(račiće)* and Dublin Bay prawns *(škampi)*. You will often see *mušule na buzaru* or *bouzara*, which means the molluscs are cooked with wine, parsley, garlic (lots) and breadcrumbs; some versions also include tomatoes. Squid *(lignji)* and octopus *(hobotnica)* also appear on most menus, cooked in a variety of ways: fried *(prigani or pržene)*, grilled *(na žaru)* or stuffed *(punjeni)*. Risotto *(rižot)* is ubiquitous, as well: *rižot plodovi mora* is a mixed seafood risotto, and *crni rižot* (black risotto) is made with squid, the rice blackened by the ink. On more upmarket menus you may find lobster *(jastog)* or oysters *(oštrige)*: the former is more prevalent on the island of Mljet, the latter up the coast in Ston and Mali Ston, where the best oysters are farmed.

The word for fish is *riba*, and varieties range from gilthead bream *(orada)*, red mullet *(trilja)* and sea bream *(arbun)* to the more humble mackerel *(skuše)*, sardines *(srdele)* and anchovies *(incuni)*, all excellent when simply grilled and served with a salad.

Above: octopus stew is a local speciality

But meat lovers should not despair. As well as the tasty Dalmatian smoked ham *(Dalmatinski pršut)*, similar to *prosciutto*, that appears as a first course on most menus, there is usually chicken breast *(pileća prsa)* or chicken escalope *(pileći file)* and pork cutlets *(svinjski kutlet)* as well as steak (simply called *biftek)*.

Vegetarians are not too well catered for, although the salads are usually fresh and ample; salad with feta cheese *(sirom)* is especially popular, and pasta with a non-meat, tomato-based sauce is usually available. Fresh vegetables *(suježe povrće)* are seasonal (which shows they are both fresh and local), and may include courgettes, aubergines and the ubiquitous Swiss chard *(blitve)*. You can often get crêpes *(palačinke)*, either savoury or sweet. And, of course, there is always pizza, which is usually very good indeed.

Although Croatians have a sweet tooth, judging by the extremely sticky, creamy cakes on sale in pastry shops *(slastičarnice)* and cafés, these are eaten as snacks, usually with coffee, and local people don't go in for puddings in a big way. You are most likely to be offered ice cream *(sladoled)*, fresh fruit *(voce)*, or *rožata*, the local version of crème caramel, which can be excellent.

What to Drink/When to Eat

As far as drinks are concerned, most of the wine you will be offered is local (or national, at least), extremely drinkable and reasonably priced. Dingač, from the Pelješac peninsula, is one of the more expensive, and regarded as one of the best, but it is a little heavy for some tastes. White wine is *bijelo vin*, red is *crno vino*. A glass of *prošek*, the dessert wine, is a pleasant way to end a meal, while *rakija (see page 68)* is for the brave. Many people drink beer *(pivo)* with meals, rather than wine. Croatian beer is tasty, inexpensive and not too high in alcohol. Dubrovnik's water *(voda)* is safe to drink and tastes fine, and most restaurants offer carafes of tap water free of charge, although they are more than happy to sell you bottled mineral water if that is what you want. Coffee *(kava)* is usually strong and good. Coffee with milk is *kava s mlijekom*; if you want it black ask for *kava* or *espreso*.

Local people usually eat lunch around 1.30pm and dinner at about 9pm, but restaurateurs are so used to catering to foreign visitors, who provide most of their trade, that they will serve lunch from midday throughout most of the afternoon, and dinner from round 6pm. Many restaurants carry on serving dinner until about 11pm.

Price guide:
Approximate prices are based on a two-course meal for two, with a bottle of house wine.
€   under 300 kn
€€   300–500 kn
€€€   over 500 kn
(Note that bb after a street name means the premises are unnumbered.)

Old Town
Amoret
Od Pustjerne bb
Tel: 020-323 739
With tables directly opposite the Cathedral as well as on a small terrace and dining room up a flight of steps, Amoret serves large helpings of fish and seafood and the service is swift and cheerful. €€

Defne
Pucić Palace Hotel
Od Puča 1
Tel: 020-326 200/222

Right: red wine from Pelješac

A roof-terrace restaurant, smart without being stuffy. Some dishes have a Middle Eastern flavour, and there is also plenty of fish, including lobster with black risotto. €€€

Domino Steak House
Od Domina 3
Tel: 020-323 103
Domino, close to the church of the same name, has been going for years and provides good-value meals on a terrace in a small square. Along with the steaks it has plenty of seafood dishes. €€

Dubrovački Kantun
Boškovićeva 5
Tel: 020-331 991/321 123
A pleasant, unpretentious little place, with friendly staff, just off Stradun. Makes good use of locally grown vegetables and serves an excellent beef stew. €€

Ekvinocijo
Ilije Sarake 10
Tel: 020-323 633
In a quiet corner tucked beneath the walls on the south side of town, this little restaurant

promises fresh local ingredients and vegetarian options. €–€€

Kamenica
Gundulićeva Poljana 8
Tel: 020-421 499/323 682
Long-established restaurant that serves food at tables outside in this busy square. Mostly fish – the grilled squid is particularly good – and they also specialise in oysters, after which the restaurant is named. €–€€

Lokanda Peskarija
Na Ponti (Old Port) bb
Tel: 020-324 750
Open from 8am until midnight in summer, this small, efficient place, with tables spread out over the Old Port jetty, has a very short menu featuring fish and seafood, brought to the table in sizzling, blackened pots, accompanied by carafes of house wine and large, no-nonsense salads. A good atmosphere and good prices. €

Mea Culpa
Za Rokom 3
Tel: 020-323 430
The biggest and best pizzas in town served at wooden benches in a narrow street parallel to Stradun. Don't be afraid to ask for one to share – they are large enough. Resist the pleading eyes of the resident cats if you are strong-minded enough. €

Poklisar
Ribarnica 1 (Old Port)
Tel: 020-322 176
Pizzas and fish dishes right beside the harbour where, at lunchtime, you can watch competing vendors of boat trips plying for trade. The atmosphere is cheerful, there's live music some evenings, and it seems to keep going until around midnight if there are customers. €€

Proto
Siroka 1
Tel: 020-323 234
Established in 1886 and still going strong, Proto, just off Stradun at the Pile Gate end, serves reliably good meat and fish at pavement tables, indoors or (mot popular) on an upstairs terrace. Book in high season. €€€

Left: refreshment break in the sun

Ragusa II
Zamanjina 2 (just off Prijeko)
Tel: 020-321 203
The Prijeko area is not the best place to eat (anywhere that touts so openly for custom is best avoided), but Ragusa has been here since 1929, so it must be doing something right. €–€€

Ribar
Damjane Jude
Tel: 091 537 2418
A friendly place, close to the Aquarium, the Ribar has been run by the Kovacic family for years. They specialise in fish, but there are also good meat dishes on offer. €–€€

Rozarij
Marija Sjekavika 4 (corner of Prijeko)
Tel: 020-423 791
The best of the Prijeko restaurants, close to the Dominican Monastery and named after the little Rozarij church next door. Serves excellent Dalmatian food in a cosy dining room or at a few tables in a shady corner outside. As it's not very big, it's a good idea to book. €€

Spaghetteria Toni
Božidarevićeva 14
Tel: 020-323 134
Just off Od Puča, this is the place for large helpings of inexpensive and very well cooked pasta, served with a wide variety of sauces. It's a place where you'll see at least as many local people as tourists, which sometimes makes a nice change. €

Ploče
Maesosto
Hvarska
Tel: 020-420 986
Popular place just outside the Ploče Gate. There is a view of the harbour if you are sitting in the right place, but you are separated from it by a busy road. However, the standard of both food and service is fine. €€

Revelin Club
Sv. Dominika bb
Tel: 178 3033 (mobile)
This is really just a café-bar (with a late-night disco) but it has been included because its terrace, overlooking the Old Port and City Walls, makes it a delightful place for a pizza or sandwich, or just a drink, and nobody seems to mind if you sit here for hours. €

Pile
Nautika
Brsalje 3
Tel: 020-442 526
The Atlas Club Nautika, to give it its full name, is still making much of having served lunch to Pope John Paul II on his last visit in July 2003. It is in a wonderful situation, just outside the Pile Gate, and overlooking Fort Lovrijenac. There are two terraces and an elegant dining room. The food and service are fit for a pope, but a bit formal, per-

Above: you won't find a table any closer to the sea than this

haps, for lesser mortals. There is also an inexpensive 'light lunch' offered on one of the terraces between noon and 4pm. Booking recommended (not necessary for the 'light lunch'). €€€

Orhan
Od Tabakarije 1 (just outside Pile Gate)
Tel: 020-414 183/891 267
Hidden away by the water's edge, beneath Fort Lovrijenac, Orhan serves excellent fish and seafood indoors or outside on a small, vine-draped terrace. Best to book in high season. €€–€€€

Posat
Uz Posat 1 (just outside Pile Gate)
Tel: 020-421 194
The setting, fronting a car park, is unprepossessing, but once you are settled on the upper terrace your view is over Fort Lovrijenac. The home-cooked food is good, especially some innovative lobster dishes. €€

Sesame
Dante Alighieri bb
Tel: 020-412 910
This pleasant little establishment is in a narrow street off the main Ante Starčevića road leading west from Pile Gate. Open for breakfast, lunch and dinner. It's popular with students, as one of the university faculties is nearby, and it has a nice local feel about it. Also has rooms for rent. €

Gruž
Bistro Riva
Lapadska Obala 20
Tel: 020-356 033
Right beside Gruž Harbour (on the Lapad side), this small, friendly place is easy to miss as it hides behind a walled courtyard. This

shelters it from the main road but also, unfortunately, from a view of the bay. However, in an area that's short of restaurants, it's a good lunchtime stop for inexpensive fish, pasta, salads, etc. Same management as the Domino in the Old Town, so they know what they are doing. €

Orsan Yacht Club
Ivana Zajca 2
Tel: 020-435 933/411 880
Slightly further up the harbourside, but right on the bay, the Orsan (the name means boathouse) serves the usual fish and rice dishes, right on the jetty – and you won't feel unwelcome because you haven't got a yacht moored nearby. €€

Lapad and Babin Kuk
Despite the number of hotels on these two peninsulas, there are relatively few restaurants. This may be because many hotels provide half-board accommodation, and most visitors don't venture outside to eat.

Casa-Bar
Nika i Meda Pucića 1
Tel: 020-435 353
Right on Lapad Bay, beneath the Villa Wolff hotel (to which it belongs), Casa is a café rather than a restaurant, but the snacks and light meals taste all the better because the view is so glorious. Pop next door to the internet outlet to check your emails. €

Komin
Iva Dulcica 136
Tel: 020-435 636
Unless you are staying in one of the Babin Kuk hotels, or enjoying the walk around the peninsula described in Route 6, you are unlikely to stumble across this place, but it's

close to the terminus of the No 6 bus. Set in a family-oriented little park, it specialises in grilled meat and fish, as the smells wafting on the breeze will indicate. €€

Konoba Konavoka
Šetaliste Kralja Zvonimira 38
Tel: 020-435 105
In the pedestrianised street lined with bars and cafés that leads down to the sea. The fishing-tackle motif on the covered terrace may be a bit overdone, but the food is good (especially the seafood risotto), and the service is prompt and friendly. €€

Levanat
Nika i Meda Pucića 15
Tel: 020-435 352
Follow the seaside path from the Casa-Bar *(see opposite)* and you will come to this delightful place. Prawns in honey with sage and salmon carpaccio are among the more unusual dishes, but standards such as stuffed squid and mussel *bouzara* are excellent, too. Or you can just have a drink and watch the sun set over the sea. €€€

Lopud
Bistro Glavovic
Obala I. Kuljevana bb
Tel: 020-759 050/359
Right on the harbourside, this is a good choice for lunch, although not the cheapest place in town. €€€

Konoba Peggy
Narikla 22
Tel: 020-759 036
Just a few metres from the harbour, this is a popular spot with a large leafy terrace and substantial helpings of fish and seafood. It can get busy, as day-trippers are often pointed in this direction and may arrrive in a bunch. €

Obala
Obala I. Kuljevana 18
Tel: 020-759 170
There are tables so close to the water you could almost dip your toes in as you eat. There is also a covered terrace and an indoor dining area. Fish couldn't be fresher and the salads are great too, especially when washed down with local wine. €€

Koločep
Villa Ruža
Donje Čelo
Tel: 020-757 030
This place is housed in a lovely stone building, set in a pine-shaded garden at the far end of the seaside promenade. The food's good, too. Open for lunch only (most visitors come here on day trips). €€

Cavtat
Dalmacija
Trumbiev put 9
Tel: 020-478 018
Set in a busy little triangle at the southern end of the harbour promenade, the popular Dalmacija has been in business since 1979. As you would expect from the name, it offers Dalmatian cooking, mainly fish but also good meat dishes, and is usually bustling and busy at lunchtime. €€

Left: ripe cherries fill market stalls in summer
Above: grilled fish and salad – simple but good

Konoba Ivan
Uvala Tiha 5
Tel: 020-478 160/478 485
On the other side of the peninsula (but only a few hundred metres if you go across the narrow neck). Konoba Ivan is a small, cheerful place right by the water's edge where fresh fish and grilled meat, accompanied by carafes of house wine, make a good lunch, especially if you've made the circuitous walk described in Excursion 3 *(see page 54)*. €

Leut
Trumbiev put 11
Tel: 020-478 477
Leut trumps its neighbour (the Dalmacija) in the longevity stakes, having been here, run by the same family, since 1971. It enjoys its reputation as Cavtat's premier restaurant, and both the food and the location are great. Reservations are advisable for weekends and high season, especially for Sunday lunch. €€€

Mljet
Bourbon
Polače 8, Polače
Tel: 020-744 142
In a row of restaurants on the harbourside, with a huge, wood-fuelled barbecue on the terrace. Like most of Mljet's restaurants it specialises in lobster – at a price. Other dishes are far more reasonable. €€

Konoba Galija
Pomena 7, Pomena
Tel: 020-744 029
One of a string of little restaurants that have opened recently along Pomena's harbourside (facing the Hotel Odisej across the bay), Galija has tables in a leafy arbour and live lobsters swimming in a huge tank. Also has accommodation. €

Melita
Sveta Marija
Tel: 020-744 145
In the remains of the monastery on St Mary's Island, Melita serves lunch, including good crêpes. If you are staying overnight on the island and want dinner you should book. €€

Stella Maris
Polače 8, Polače
Tel: 020-744 059

Above: eating out in the Old Town on a warm summer's evening

Another Polače restaurant with a harbour-front site, this one so close to the ferry dock that you could sit here until the gangplank is about to go up. Offers the usual seafood and grilled meat dishes along with local wine and friendly service. €€

Korčula
Hotel Korčula
Obala Franje Tudjman bb
Tel: 020-711 078
The hotel restaurant has an elegant dining room and a pretty vine-covered terrace opposite the ferry dock. There's an extensive list of local wines to accompany the excellent fish dishes. €€€

Kanavelić
Sv. Barabare 15
Tel: 020-711 800
Set in the old walled town, and named after 17th-century poet Petar Kanavelić, who was born here, the restaurant is known for its well-prepared fish dishes. €€

Mali Ston
All the restaurants in little Mali Ston specialise in the oysters and mussels that are cultivated here, and of which they are very proud. They are the reason people flock here for Sunday lunch, but the venues also serve a range of other seafood and fish, and some meat dishes.

Bota Šare
Tel: 020-754 482
Cavernous, stone-walled dining room and lots of outside tables on a waterside terrace. The specialities, of course, are oysters, mussels and local wines; some Dalmatian meat dishes, too. €€

Villa Koruna
Mali Ston bb
Tel: 020-754 999
The best known of the Mali Ston restaurants, the Koruna has a vast, glass-covered terrace, a cosy, old-fashioned dining room, and fish swimming in large tanks (as well as two large turtles, which are not for clients' consumption). Presentation is great and the food is good, too, but no better than you get in the neighbouring eating places. €€

NIGHTLIFE

If your idea of nightlife is sitting in a pleasant café under the stars with a drink in front of you and music in the background, or listening to a classical recital in an ancient building, Dubrovnik will suit you well. If your taste veers more towards clubs and discos, you may be in the wrong place. However, there are a few places with night-time action.

Bars
Carpe Diem
Kneza Damjana Jude 4
Close to the Aquarium, the Carpe Diem is a restaurant by day but its minimalist interior becomes a cocktail bar in the evening and stays open late.

Hemingway Bar
Pred Dvorom
Opposite the Rector's Palace, the Hemingway has little to do with its famous namesake, but it does have comfy padded armchairs and innovative cocktails.

Jazz Caffé Troubadur
Bunićeva Poljana
A tiny place with loads of atmosphere and chairs and tables outside in the square. It has live jazz nearly every night in summer, starting about 9.30pm. The service is excellent, and while the drinks are a bit pricier than elsewhere, you do get entertainment thrown in.

Clubs
Eastwest
Banje Beach, Ploče
Just outside the Ploče Gate (by the Lazareti), the Eastwest Beach club has music and cocktails into the early hours.

Exodus
Babin Kuk
At the other end of town and the other end of the spectrum, the large Exodus Club, part of the hotel complex at Babin Kuk, offers techno music for a young crowd.

Lazareti
Frana Supila 8
www.clubpages.net
Hosts live bands and top DJs.

Latin Club Fuego
Brsalje 11, Pile
A popular spot for Latin music, Thur–Sat till 4am, just outside Pile Gate.

Classical Music

Throughout the summer, classical concerts are held in a number of different venues, preceding and following the Dubrovnik Festival *(see below)*. The Dubrovnik String Quartet and the Sorkorčević Quartet give recitals on Sunday, Monday and Wednesday evening in the church of **Our Saviour** (beside the Franciscan Monastery). The Domino Quartet performs in the **Domino Church** (Od Domino, just off Stradun) on Saturday evening. The Dubrovnik Symphony Orchestra gives full-scale concerts occasionally in the **Revelin Fortress** and frequently in the atrium of the **Rector's Palace** (check with the tourist office and the prominent advertisements outside the palace for dates). The Rector's Palace concerts usually start at 9pm, and tickets can be purchased in advance. The other recitals usually begin at 9.30pm, and tickets can only be bought at the door from one hour before the performance. Flaming torches are placed outside the venue where an event is being held.

Folk Music

The **Lindo Ensemble**, highly esteemed throughout Croatia, perform folk dance and song in an outdoor venue in the **Lazareti** on summer evenings (bilboards all over town give details). A highly polished professional troupe and the costumes are stunning. If you like folk music, you'll love this. There is a phone number for advance bookings (tel: 020-323 535), but most tickets are sold at the door, from an hour before the performance.

There are also folk dance performances on Sunday morning in Luža Square and in the village of Čilipi (near the airport). Public transport to Čilipi is not good, but various tour agencies in the town run organised coach trips.

FESTIVALS

There are two major festivals in Dubrovnik: the celebrations for St Blaise's day on 2–3 February, and the Summer Libertas Festival in July and August.

The Festival of St Blaise

You can't be in Dubrovnik for long without realising that St Blaise (Sveti Vlaho) is the city's patron saint. Not only does his image (carrying a scale model of the town) appear over the Pile and Ploče gates, and on other public buildings, but he has his own church, in the centre of the Old City, and his relics are kept in the Cathedral Treasury. Martyred in the 3rd century, Blaise was an Armenian bishop, whose remains were brought to Dubrovnik in 972. Shortly afterwards, as legend has it, he appeared in a vision to a local priest warning that the Venetians were about to attack the city. The attack was repelled and Blaise became the city's patron. The saint's day is 3 February – a great day in Dubrovnik. The festival is ceremonially opened the preceding day at 3.30pm outside St Blaise's church, and at 10am on the day a celebratory

Mass is held in front of the Cathedral, followed by a procession around the town, led by church dignitaries, that carries the saint's relics under a red canopy. The town is decked with flags and banners and the whole population, it seems, along with people from surrounding areas, join in. Many of them carry hand-made banners and dress in the national costume that you normally only see at folkdance displays. The ceremony culminates in the bishop blessing them all before releasing three white doves. Festivities continue through the day with music, dancing and lively family meals.

Summer Festival

Dubrovnik's Summer Festival, inaugurated in 1950, lasts for around six weeks from early July to late August. It is a wonderful time to be in the city, but you need to book accommodation well in advance or you will have little chance of finding a room.

Performances are staged in prestigious venues all over the city, and offerings may vary from classical Indian dance and performances by English guitarist John Williams in the Revelin Fortress, to a staging of *Ham let* in the dramatic setting of Fort Lovrijenac. The Marin Držić theatre and adjoining Bursa Theatre stage dramatic and musical performances, including a number by Držić himself, the city's favourite 16th-century playwright. Numerous concerts are held in the beautiful atrium of the Rector's Palace, from performances by the resident Dubrovnik Symphony Orchestra to chamber recitals by the Borodin and Bartok Quartets. The Domino Church and the Church of Our Saviour are other venues for chamber music, as they are throughout the summer. Then there are the streets of the Old Town itself, where the Natural Theatre Company performs, music is played, flaming torches burn, and costumed figures add to the atmosphere.

For details, tel: 020-326 100, fax: 020-326 116, e-mail:info@dubrovnik-festival.hr, or check the programme and venues online at www.dubrovnik-festival.hr.

There is also the annual **Libertas International Film Festival** which has been going since 2003 and is held usually during the last week of June. For further information e-mail info@libertasfilmfestival.com.

CALENDAR OF EVENTS

2–3 February: celebrations in honour of Sveti Vlaho (St Blaise) *(see previous page)*.

Mid- to late February: Carnival, with colourful processions in Stradun and masked balls in the large hotels. Processions are also held in Cavtat.

March–April. Good Friday processions. Easter Sunday: processions after Mass and the blessing of the town at the land and sea gates.

Late May: International Film Festival.

Mid-June: Corpus Christi celebrated with Mass and street processions.

Mid-June: Lapad Yacht Regatta, an event lasting two days.

22 June: Anti-Fascist Resistance Day, a national holiday.

late June: Libertas Film Festival Festival.

Mid-July–late August: Libertas, Dubrovnik Summer Festival *(see above)*.

July–August: Cavtat Summer Festival: male voice choirs and water polo tournaments.

29 July: St Theodor's Day in Korčula is celebrated with the Moreska (Sword Dance Festival), basically a battle between good and evil *(see Excursion 5, page 64)*. A colourful, ritualised event, which garners huge local support, with brass bands playing the battle march. It is believed to originate from the Moors and Christians festivals held in many parts of Spain.

Early August: Southern Dalmatia Yacht Regatta, a two-day event.

15 August: Feast of the Assumption.

Late September–early October: grape harvest festival in Pelješac and Korčula.

8 October: Independence Day.

Late October: Semper Primus Rowing Regatta, Gruž Harbour.

1 November: All Saints' Day. Local people buy flowers in the markets to take to the tombs of family and friends, where candles are lit as darkness falls.

24 December: family feasts and Midnight Mass.

25–26 December: Christmas, two-day national holiday.

31 December: New Year celebrated with fireworks at midnight in Stradun.

(Also see Public Holidays, page 85.)

Left: you can see folk dancers at the Lazareti, and in Luža Square and Čilipi on Sunday mornings in summer

Practical Information

GETTING THERE

By Air

Most visitors fly to Dubrovnik. From the UK, flights take about 2 hour 40 minutes. In summer there are frequent direct flights with British Airways (tel: 0870-850 9850, www. britishairways.com), Croatia Airlines (tel: 020-8563 0022, www.croatiaairlines.hr) and easyJet (www.easyjet.com). Return flight prices in high summer range from £160–450; out of season (May/September/October) they can drop to £120; in winter they may be even cheaper but you may have to go via Zagreb or Vienna, making it a long journey. However, BA runs a direct winter service three times a week. Also check www.opodo. com and www.expedia.co.uk. There are a number of charter flights, too, and many companies arrange good flight and accommodation packages, and they don't always mean you will end up in a big package-holiday hotel. Simply Travel (tel: 0871-231 4050, www.simplytravel.com) and Thomsons (tel: 0871-231 4691, www.thomson.co.uk) are reliable companies.

There are no direct flights from Australia, Canada or the US, but flights via London or other European airports are not hard to arrange, and most long-distance passengers come to Dubrovnik as part of a trip to Europe.

Dubrovnik's airport (Zranča Luka; tel: 020-773 333/377) is at Čilipi, about 20km (12 miles) south. Atlas Travel Agency runs a bus service between the airport and the main bus station that connects with the arrival of scheduled flights (35 kuna), but otherwise you will have to take a taxi (around 250 kuna at 2009 rates). If you have a flight-and-accommodation package you will be met at the airport.

There are banks and exchange facilities, car hire outlets and duty-free shops on site.

By Sea

You can reach Dubrovnik by sea from Bari on a direct ferry run by Jadrolinija. In high season they run Tuesday to Sunday at 10pm, arriving in Dubrovnik at 7am the next day, but timetables may change (tel: 385 51-666 111, www.jadrolinija.hr). Ferries arrive in Gruž Harbour, a five-minute walk from the Libertas bus station (see page 83). Azzurra Line (Bari: tel: +39 080-592 8400, Dubrovnik: tel: 020-313 178, www.azzurraline.com) makes three weekly crossings in summer.

By Bus

You can get to Dubrovnik by bus from London's Victoria Station, but it takes about 48 hours and is not much cheaper than some flights (for details, tel: 08717-818 181, www.eurolines.com).

By Car

Unless you are visiting Dubrovnik as part of an extended tour of Croatia, travelling by car is not a good option. Cars are not allowed into the Old City and parking in the new town can be difficult. However, if you do travel by car try to find a hotel with private parking, and leave your car there when you arrive, or stay outside town in Cavtat or Zaton and makes trips in by bus or boat.

If you are driving, remember to drive on the right and stick to the speed limits of 130kph (80mph) on motorways, 100kph (62mph) on dual carriageways, 50kph (30mph) in built-up areas and 80kph (50mph) outside built-up areas, or you could risk a heavy fine. You need a national or international driving licence and you should carry your passport as proof of identity at all times. EU nationals do not need a green card. (For car hire, see page 84.)

TRAVEL ESSENTIALS

Visas and Passports

Citizens of EU countries, and those from Australia, New Zealand, the US and Canada, need only a valid passport to visit Croatia for stays of up to three months. If you are going

Left: weather-worn tiles on a Dubrovnik roof

on day trips to Bosnia-Herzegovina or Montenegro you need to take your passport with you, but you don't need a visa.

All foreign visitors are required to register with the police within 24 hours of their arrival, but in practice this is done by the hotel or owner of the private accommodation in which you are staying, and it is their responsibility, not yours, to see that it is done.

Customs

Customs regulations are in line with those of European Union countries. Foreign currency up to a value of €3,000 can be brought in and taken out of the country. Technical equipment such as laptop computers should, in theory, be registered when you arrive, but in practice customs officials do not always seem very interested. Visitors who make purchases costing more than 500 kuna may reclaim VAT (PDV) *(see Shopping, page 67, for details)*.

When to Visit

The best times to visit are May–June and September–October. The weather should be fine and sunny *(see below)* and the sea swimmable, the town will be less crowded, accommodation easier to find and flights will be cheaper. But if you like the heat and don't mind crowds it is great fun to be in Dubrovnik during the summer festival (mid-July–August), but do book accommodation well in advance. Dubrovnik can be lovely on a crisp, cold winter day, but there are wet and windy days too, you are less likely to get a direct flight, some restaurants and many hotels close, and few, if any, boats run to the islands.

Weather

Average temperatures in winter (November –February) range from 8–12°C (46–54°F), April, May and October 14–18°C (57–65°F), June and September 21–22°C (70–72°F), July–August 24–25°C (75–77°F), although summer highs can soar up to 30°C (86°F).

Clothing

Most styles of dressing are tolerated, but Croatians like to dress smartly and you will blend in more easily if you do, too. Visitors of both sexes should avoid short shorts and bare shoulders when visiting churches. Topless bathing is not actually forbidden on most beaches but it is not common. For comfort, wear loose, light clothes in summer, but remember that sudden downpours do happen, so a waterproof and umbrella are useful, as is a sweater or jacket for evenings. Flip-flop sandals, sunhats, sarongs and other beach cover-ups are easy to find when you get here.

Electricity

The standard is 220 volts. Sockets take plugs with two round pins, so UK visitors need adapters. Visitors from the US need transformers for 110-volt appliances.

Time Differences

GMT plus one hour in winter, plus two hours in summer.

GETTING ACQUAINTED

Geography

Croatia has a jagged 1,775-km (1,100-mile) Adriatic coastline. Dubrovnik is situated near the southern tip, in Southern Dalmatia, on a narrow strip of land bordered by Bosnia-Herzegovina and Montenegro. The surrounding landscape is sparsely vegetated and typified by porous limestone and *karst* rock.

Government

Under Croatia's 1990 constitution, legislative power rests with the directly elected Chamber of Representatives and the Chamber of Districts. Executive power is held by the president, who is elected for five years. The current president is Stjepan Mesić, who was elected for a second five-year term in February 2005. The prime minister is Ivo Sanader. Croatia has applied for membership of the EU and is expected to join in 2010.

Religion

Croatia is a Roman Catholic country. Dubrovnik had a registered Catholic population of 84 percent in the 2001 census, and church attendance is high. There are small Muslim and Serbian Orthodox populations and a tiny Jewish one.

Population

The population of Dubrovnik is around 44,000 (about 10,000 less than in 1990), of whom it

practical information

is estimated that only about 1,000 now live in the Old City. The vast majority are Croats, and proud to describe themselves as such.

MONEY MATTERS

Currency

Croatia's currency is the kuna (abbreviated to kn or, sometimes, HRK), which is divided into 100 lipa. There are 1, 2, 5, 10, 20, 50 lipa coins, 1, 2, 5 and 25 kuna coins and 5, 10, 20, 50, 100, 200, 500 and 1,000 kuna banknotes. A few businesses will accept euros.

Exchange

Foreign currency can be exchanged at banks, exchange bureaux, post offices and most tourist agencies and hotels. Banking hours are Monday–Friday 8am–7pm (8am–5pm for smaller branches), Saturday 8am–1pm. Cash machines (ATMs) are found throughout the city, especially in Stradun, and in Cavtat and Korčula, but are harder to find on the smaller islands. Exchange rates (2009) are about £1 sterling = 8 kuna, $1 = 6 kuna, 1€ = 7 kuna.

Credit Cards

Most hotels, restaurants and larger shops accept credit cards (American Express, Diners Club, Eurocard/Mastercard, Visa), but it is always wise to check in advance.

Taxes

All prices shown are net, ie what you actually have to pay. If you look closely you may see that an amount for VAT (PDV) is detailed on some bills, but this does not mean it is extra, as the tax is built into the price.

Tipping

Service charge is rarely added to restaurant bills, so a tip of 10 percent should be added if you are happy with the service. Taxi drivers appreciate a tip, even if you just round up the amount. Hotel porters should be tipped if they are helpful, and cleaning staff should be given an amount commensurate with your length of stay.

GETTING AROUND

Bus

Dubrovnik's bus service, run by **Libertas** (tel: 020-357 020, www.libertasdubrovnik. hr), is excellent, and unless you are out very late at night is probably the only form of transport you will need in the city. The Libertas kiosks at the bus station (Autobusni Kolodvor) on Put Republike, at the city end of Gruž Harbour and at the bus stops by Pile Gate, will provide you with an up-to-date timetable, as will the tourist office and most hotel reception desks. You can pay on the bus (exact money only, currently 10 kuna), but it's cheaper and easier to buy tickets at newsagents kiosks (there's usually one near main bus stops) or at your hotel. You can buy any number you want, pay only 8 kuna each and avoid the necessity of finding the right change. For many visitors, the No 6 is the

Above: it is safe to drink the water from the Big and Small Onofrian fountains

most useful route, as it runs from Pile Gate to Lapad and Babin Kuk, where many hotels are located. The service runs about six times an hour at peak periods, and continues until 1am (later in high summer).

Long-distance buses – to Zagreb, Zadar, Split and international destinations – run from a bus station on Gruž Harbour (past the ferry terminal; tel: 060 30 50 70).

Taxi

Taxi fares are metered and are not exorbitant. There are taxi stands outside Pile Gate (which lists prices to major destinations), outside Ploče Gate, at Gruž Harbour (in front of the Jadrolinija office) and by the bus station. Radio Taxi Dubrovnik runs a 24-hour service (tel: 020-970); and Niksa (tel: 091091 53 10022) is friendly and reliable.

Car

If you want to hire a car to make trips outside the city, you could book in advance by checking www.compare.carrentals.co.uk, which lists the best deals from a huge number of companies. **Europcar** also has an office in Dubrovnik at Kardinala Stepinca 32 (tel: 091-330 3031) and at the airport (tel: 020-773 511), **Hertz** is at Frana Supila 9 (tel: 020-425 000) and **Gulliver** (a reliable local company) is next door at Frana Supila 7 (tel: 020-462 477), while **Avi**s has a general reservations number for Croatia (tel: 062-222 226).

Boat

There are numerous boat services to the nearby islands and to Cavtat. For boats to Cavtat and Lokrum, simply turn up at the Old Port and you will have a choice of vessels of various shapes and sizes, all charging about the same fare. **Nova International** (tel: 020-313 599, www.nova-dubrovnik.hr) runs fast services between Gruž and the Old Port, from Gruž to Zaton, and from the Old Port to Cavtat and the Elaphite Islands. For the Elaphites you can book trips through a number of different agencies, who have stands on Lapad Bay and in the Old Port *(see Tour Agencies, page 91)*.

HOURS AND HOLIDAYS

Business Hours

Most shops open Mon–Sat 9am–8pm in summer, although some close on Saturday afternoon. In winter, they may close for lunch. Supermarkets stay open till 9pm and also open on Sunday. Most markets operate from around 7am until noon or 1pm. Main post offices are open Mon–Fri 8am–7pm or 8pm, Sat 8am–2pm or 4pm. Hours for larger banks are Mon–Fri 8am–7pm, Sat 8am–1pm.

Public Holidays

1 January New Year's Day
3 February Sveti Vlaho (St Blaise)
March/April Easter Monday
1 May Labour Day
June Corpus Christi (dates vary)
22 June Anti-Fascist Resistance Day
25 June Statehood Day
5 August Homeland Thanksgiving Day
15 August Feast of the Assumption
8 October Independence Day
1 November All Saints' Day
25–26 December Christmas

ACCOMMODATION

Hotels

Most of Dubrovnik's hotels are large, modern and efficient, with air conditioning, swimming pools, room service, etc. Increasingly, they are owned by a few big corporations. Many visitors to Dubrovnik come on package deals, which usually include half board accommodation, generally at a price considerably lower than the rack rates given below. Hotel rates are often quoted in euros, but charged in kuna.

There are a few smaller, more personal hotels, however, and a growing number of rooms and apartments for rent – look for signs saying *sobe* or *apartman*. The identical dark blue signs indicate that the establishment is regulated. A room in a private house usually doesn't include breakfast, so you have to go to the nearest café.

All hotel rates vary according to the time of year – there are some very good deals to be had off-season. The rates below are for a standard, en suite double room in high season (July–mid-September).

Price Guide

€€€€	over €300
€€€	€180–300
€€	€120–180
€	under €120

(Hotels are listed alphabetically by area. Note that bb after a street name means the premises are unnumbered.)

Old City

Apartments Marc & Silva van Bloemen
Bandureva 1
Tel: 020-323 433
Mobile: 098 619 282
www.karmendu.com
Three spacious and one smaller apartment in a family house right beside the harbour. Attractively decorated, with bright rugs and bedspreads, original paintings on the walls and smart, modern bathrooms. Friendly, helpful hosts with loads of local knowledge that they are happy to share. €

Family House Fascination
Od Domino 8
Tel/Fax: 020-323 112
e-mail: apartments.fascination@gmail.com
Four rooms and one studio apartment in a friendly family house in a narrow street leading up from Stradun. There's a garden and a delightful terrace. €

Pucić Palace
Od Puča 1
Tel: 020-326 222
Fax: 20-326 223
www.thepucicpalace.com
One of only two hotels in the Old City, this is the last word in discreet luxury and comfort. Set in a Renaissance palace, it offers 19 rooms and suites, of which the Gundulić Suite on the first floor, overlooking the square of the same name, is the highlight. There's a restaurant (the Dafne), a brasserie (Café Royal), 24-hour room service, a beauty centre and a library in an old chapel. The hotel also has a private yacht, available (separate charge) for trips up the coast. €€€€

Stari Grad
Od Sigurate 4
Tel: 020-322 244
Fax: 020-321 256
www.hotelstarigrad.com
This small three-star hotel (only eight rooms) occupies an aristocratic family house, a tall narrow building just off Stradun. Furnished with antiques, it has a café-bar on the ground floor and a rooftop terrace for breakfast in summer. No lift. €€€

Ploče

Excelsior Hotel
Frana Supila 12
Tel: 020-353 353
Fax: 020-353 295
www.alh.hr
A large, luxurious hotel with splendid sea and Old City views, around five minutes' walk from the Ploče Gate. The hotel originates from 1913 and was fully renovated in 1998. Spa, fitness centre, steam bath and indoor pool; piano bar and restaurant. €€€€

Grand Villa Argentina
Frana Supila 14
Tel: 020-440 555
Fax: 020-432 524
www.gva.hr

Left: numerous boat trips run from the Old Port

About five minutes' walk from Ploče Gate, this hotel is in a beautiful setting, amid pine and palm trees, overlooking the sea, with views of Lokrum and the Old City. There's a private beach, indoor and outdoor pools, sauna, gym and an attractive restaurant terrace. The older part of the hotel dates from 1922, and there is a smart, modern six-storey wing. All floors are served by a lift, but access to the hotel and to the beach make it unsuitable for people with restricted mobility. €€€€

Villa Dubrovnik
Vlaha Bukovka 6
Tel: 020-422 933
Fax: 020-423 465
www.villa-dubrovnik.hr
The lovely old hotel has been demolished and a smart new one, with all mod cons, is supposedly due to open for the 2010 season. The setting is incomparable. €€€

Villa Orsula
Frana Supila 14
Tel: 020-440 555
Fax: 020-432 524
www.gva.com
Part of the Villa Argentina complex, set in an attractive stone-built villa with gardens leading down to the sea. Twelve rooms and three suites (all the doubles have sea views). There's a restaurant with a terrace, and a café in the garden. Use of Villa Argentina's gym and spa facilities. €€€€

Pile
Hotel Bellevue
Pera Cingrije 7
Tel: 020-330 000
Fax: 020-330 100
www.hotel-bellevue.hr
Boutique hotel built into the cliff overlooking Dance Bay. Each of the 93 rooms has a sea view. Lots of local wood and stone have been used in the design, and rooms feaure paintings by prestigious Croatian artists. Good restaurant and all the facilities you would expect. €€€€

Hilton Imperial Hotel
Marijana Blazica 2
Tel: 020-320 320
Fax: 020-320 220
www.hilton.com
Despite the address, the hotel fronts onto Branitelja Dubrovnika, the road leading uphill from the Pile Gate. It combines two late 19th-century hotels and aims to preserve their atmosphere while offering all mod cons. Wood and marble finishes give a luxurious air. There's a large terrace, restaurant, piano bar, indoor pool and gym. €€€€

Hotel Lero
Iva Vojnovića 14
Tel: 020-341 333
Fax: 020-332 123
www.hotel-lero.hr
On the main road between Pile and Lapad, the Lero is a rather dull block of a hotel, but has been recently modernised, and has a good location, approximately 200 metres/yards from the beach, and on the frequent No 6 bus route. About half the rooms have sea views and it represents very good value. €€

Left: Hilton Imperial Hotel

Gruž

Hotel Lapad

Lapadska Obala 37
Tel: 020-455 570/455 555
Fax: 020-455 551
www.hotel-lapad.hr

An attractive 19th-century building with a modern wing on the Lapad side of Gruž Harbour, 3km (2 miles) from the Pile Gate and on a bus route. Rooms in the new wing have air conditioning. There's a pool and a boat service to the nearest beach in summer. €€

Hotel Petka

Obala Stjepana Radića 38
Tel: 020-410 500
Fax: 020-410 127
www.hotelpetka.com

Close to the ferry port, this functional hotel, renovated in 2008, is good value. Get a room with a harbour view and balcony if you can. On a regular bus route into the Old City. €€

Lapad

Hotel Dubrovnik

Šetalište Kralje Zvonimira bb
Tel: 020-435 030/435 033
Fax: 020-435 999
www.hoteldubrovnik.hr

A friendly, no-frills hotel on a popular pedestrianised street just a few minutes' walk from the beach; 15 ensuite rooms and six suites, all have air conditioning and satellite TV. €€

Dubrovnik Palace

Masarykov put 20
Tel: 020-430 000/430 100
Fax: 020-437 285
www.dubrovnikpalace.hr

The Dubrovnik Palace, recently refurbished, dominates the Lapad headland. All the 307 rooms have sea views and balconies and the ground-floor bar (one of several) has a wall of glass directly over the sea. There are three pools and various restaurants, along with the Dubrava conference centre. €€€€

Hotel Komodor

Masarykov put 5
Tel: 020-433 500
Fax: 020-433 510
www.hotelimaestral.com

The first in a row of five hotels in this street along the side of Lapad Bay, all part of the Maestral chain. It is the oldest and most traditional of the five but has recently been refurbished. Restaurant and outdoor pool. €€

Hotel Kompas

Šetalište Kralje Zvonimira 56
Tel: 020-352 000
Fax: 020-435 877
www.hotel-kompas.hr

Despite the street address, the Kompas fronts onto Lapad Bay. Recently upgraded, it is smart and modern, with indoor and outdoor pools, restaurant, air conditioning, satellite TV, lifts to all floors. Live music on the terrace is very loud and rather cheesy, but the atmosphere is cheerful. €€–€€€

Hotel Splendid

Masarykov put 10
Tel: 020-433 560
Fax: 020-433 570
www.hotelimaestral.com

Another in the Maestral chain, this one backing straight onto the beach and bay. Impersonal but comfortable and efficient. €€–€€€

Hotel Uvala

Masarykov put 10
Tel: 020-433 890
Fax: 020-433 591
www.hotelimaestral.com

The newest in the Maestral group has a Wellness Centre and offers all kinds of spa, massage and fitness services. It's the smartest of the five, with minimalist décor, indoor and outdoor pools and excellent service. Macrobiotic dishes on the restaurant menu. €€€
(The Hotel Vis and the Adriatic are the other two hotels on the bay in this chain. Check the above website for details.)

Hotel Zagreb

Šetalište Kralje Zvonimira 27
Tel: 020-436 333
Fax: 020-436 006

A comfortable, traditional hotel, renovated in 2005, in an attractive terracotta-coloured building set in palm-shaded gardens. Its dining room has a glassed-in terrace. All rooms air conditioned; no lift. Less than five minutes' walk from the beach and approximately two minutes' from a bus stop. €€

practical information

Villa Wolff

Nika i Meda Pučića 1
Tel: 020-438 710
Fax: 020-356 432
www.villa-wolff.hr

An elegant boutique hotel with stunning views across the bay and a pleasant palm tree-shaded terrace on which to have breakfast. Internet access in all rooms. The Casa-Bar by the water's edge *(see page 74)* is part of the hotel. No pool, but safe swimming from the rocks immediately below. €€€

Babin Kuk
Hotel Argosy

Iva Dulčića 41
Tel: 020-446 100
Reservation centre: (385) 52 465 400
www.valamar.com

A member of the Valamar Babin Kuk complex, the Argosy is more down-market than the Dubrovnik President *(see below)*, but has wonderful views, an outdoor pool and a programme of children's activities, making it a good choice for families. €€

Dubrovnik President

Iva Dulčića 39
Tel: 020-441 100
Reservation centre: (385) 52 465 400
www.valamar.com

This large hotel (163 rooms) commands the headland, facing out to sea like a great ship. It is the senior partner of the Valamar Babin Kuk complex, comprising five establishments. All rooms have balconies and sea views, and there are tennis courts, a gym, etc. External lifts take guests down to the hotel's rocky beaches. €€€
(The other hotels in the complex are the Tirena and the Valamar Club and, opening in 2009, the Valamar Lacroma Resort; see website above for details.)

Importanne Resort

Kardinala Stepinça 31
Tel: 020-440 100
Fax: 020-440 200
www.importanneresort.com

The other major player on the Babin Kuk peninsula, this group includes the **Neptun,** the **Ariston**, **Importanne Suites** and the **Villa Elita** – extremely elite and expensive. The Neptun has a restaurant/café terrace that offers one of the best places in Dubrovnik to watch the sun go down. €€€ Villa Elita €€€€
(See website above for details.)

Cavtat
Hotel Croatia

Frankopanska 10
Cavtat 20210
Tel: 020-475 555/478 150
www.hoteli-croatia.hr

Above: Lapad Bay is lined with hotels

On a peninsula to the south of the village, the Croatia, renovated in 2008, is a big, modern hotel, popular with tour agencies. Sailing, large pool, mini-golf, tennis, children's activities. Great views, but a bit of a hike down to the beach. €€€

Hotel Supetar

Ante Starčevića 27
Tel: 020-479 833
Fax: 020-479 858
www.hoteli-croatia.hr/supetar

A comfortable hotel in a traditional stone building right by the bay, the Supetar has 28 rooms, a restaurant, bar and breakfast terrace with wonderful views. Friendly staff. €€

Hotel Villa Kvaternik

Kvaternikova 3
Tel: 020-479 800
Fax: 020-479 808
www.hotelvillakvaternik.com

Five rooms and a suite in a 15th-century building with a courtyard tucked behind the Franciscan Monastery, just off the bay. Personal friendly service from the the owners, who came here from Australia in 2002. As of 2005 there are also eight simple rooms available in the former monastery. €€

Lopud
Hotel Villa Vilina

Obala Iva Kuljevana 5
Tel: 020-759 333
Fax: 020-759 060
www.villa-vilina.hr

In an historic, well-furnished family house by the harbour, the Vilina has 14 rooms and three suites, air-conditioning, and an excellent restaurant that includes fruit and olives from the garden on its menu. Friendly, personable service. At the upper end of the price range. €€

Korčula
Hotel Korčula

Šetalište F. Kršinića 102
Tel: 020-726 336
Fax: 020-711 746

The elegant Korčula hotel, right by the harbour, has 20 rooms and four apartments, a lovely vine-shaded terrace, a good restaurant and wood panelled public areas. €€–€€€

Mali Ston
Hotel Vila Koruna

Tel: 020-754 999
Mobile: 098 344 233
Fax: 020-754 642
www.vilakoruna.cjb.net

Famous as Mali Ston's oldest restaurant and purveyor of local oysters, the Vila Koruna has comfortable, functional rooms and a pleasant indoor restaurant as well as the large glass terrace overlooking the bay. €

HEALTH & EMERGENCIES

There are no particular health hazards in Croatia, and no vaccinations are required. Some visitors may experience mild stomach upsets due to unfamiliar food, but most problems, in high summer, are due to too much sun – dehydration or sunburn. Remember to drink plenty of water, use a high-factor sunblock and wear a hat. Dubrovnik's tap water is safe to drink and it tastes fine, but bottled water *(vodo)* is widely available if you prefer it.

Mosquitoes can be a problem in summer, so take protective cream or lotion and perhaps invest in an appliance that plugs into a socket in your hotel room.

Remember to take out health insurance before you leave home, in case of illness or accident. This usually comes as part of a general travel insurance package. Theoretically, citizens of EU countries should get free hospital care, but this should not be relied on. But take your EHIC (European Health Insurance Card) with you, as it might come in useful.

Dubrovnik's **hospital** is in Lapad at Roka Mišetića, tel: 020-431 777, and has a 24-hour emergency department (tel: 94).

There is also the **Policlinic**, at Ante Starčevića 45, tel: 020-416 866; open Monday–Friday 8am–8.30pm, Saturday 8am–1pm. The clinic also has a dental service (tel: 020-412 433), Monday–Friday 7am–9.30pm, Saturday 7am–noon. There is also a dental surgery at Kvaternika 14, tel: 020-332 644.

Hotel receptionists will be able to advise you about medical and dental services for non-urgent matters.

practical information

Pharmacies

There are pharmacies *(ljekarne)* all over the city. Main ones include:
• Ljekarna Gruž, Gruška Obala, tel: 020-418 990; open Monday–Friday 8am–8pm, Saturday 8am–3pm.
• Ljekarna Kod Zvonika, Placa, tel: 020-428 656; open Monday–Friday 8am–8pm, Saturday 8am–3pm.
• Ljekarna Kod Male Braće, Placa, Placa tel: 020-426 372; open Monday–Friday 8am–8.30pm, Saturday 8am–1.30pm.
• Ljekarna Lapad, M.Vodopića 30, tel: 020-436 788; open Monday–Friday 8am–8pm, Saturday 8am–3pm.
    Kod Zvonika and Gruž are the rota chemists on duty alternately outside the above hours, but only 7.30am–8pm.

Emergency Numbers

Ambulance and Medical Emergency: 94
Fire-service: 93
Police: 92
Assistance on the roads: 987

Crime

Dubrovnik is, on the whole, a safe city, and crime rates are low. As elsewhere, of course, take care of your property, keep an eye on your luggage, and don't flash large sums of money around. If you are a victim of a crime, report it to the police (tel: 92). You will need a police report, made within 24 hours, if you want to make an insurance claim. Women travellers do not usually experience harrassment here, and anyone making unwanted advances will generally take a firm no for an answer.

COMMUNICATIONS & MEDIA

Post

The main post offices *(pošta)* are in Siroka 8 (off Stradun), open Monday–Friday 8am–7pm, Saturday 8am–2pm; and Put Republike 32 (near the bus station), open Monday–Friday 8am–8pm, Saturday 8am–4pm. Stamps are sold in post offices and in some shops that sell postcards (as long as you buy your postcards there). It usually takes about two weeks for a postcard to get from Dubrovnik to another European destination, but can be faster.

Phones

The telephone code for Croatia is 385; the code for Dubrovnik and the rest of Southern Dalmatia is 020. The international access code is 00, followed by the country code (+44 for the UK, +1 for the US and Canada, +61 for Australia). Public phones can be used only with phone cards, which can be purchased in post offices and at newsagents' kiosks, and in many hotels. You can make international calls from a phone box but it may be preferable to phone from a post office where you make your call then pay afterwards.
International operator: 901
International directory enquiries: 902
Local directory enquiries: 988

Internet

There are numerous internet cafés and offices in Dubrovnik, and many hotels also offer internet access. Among the outlets are:
Internet Centar, Branitelja Dubrovnika 7 (in the tourist office), mobile tel: 099 4771 777, which has the cheapest rates.
The Netcafe, Prijeko 21, tel: 020-321 025, www.netcafe.hr.
Internet Park, Šetalište Kralje Zvonimira 56, Lapad, tel: 020-356 894, 'every sunny day'. Claims to be the world's only internet park 'where computers grow under the trees'.

Media

The newspaper you will see most frequently is the *Feral Tribune* (which at a quick glance can be mistaken for the *Herald Tribune*), a paper with a reputation for opposing the government. Editions of international newspapers are available from many news kiosks and shops, usually a day or two late.
    The BBC World Service is obtainable on a short-wave radio, but most foreign visitors get their news via the satellite television, available in the majority of hotel rooms.

Right: planning the route

TOUR AGENCIES

There are a number of tour agencies that organise trips to the Elaphite Islands, to Korčula, Ston and the Pelješac peninsula, to the Neretva River delta, to Mljet, and further afield to Montenegro, Mostar, Sarajevo and other destinations.

Atlas (www.atlas-croatia.com), the best known, has been here since Dubrovnik was still part of Yugoslavia, and has its main office just outside the Pile Gate (Sv. Durda 1, tel: 020-442 574/442 585, information line: tel: 0800 44 22 22). The firm also has machines scattered around town from which you can book trips and buy tickets. **Elite Travel** (Vukovarska 17, tel: 020-358 301, www.elite.hr) runs a similar programme with similar prices and does day cruises on the lovely galleon *Tirena*. **Amico Tours** (Od. Skara 1, tel: 020-418 248, is a newer outfit, with an interesting programme; and **Globtour Dubrovnik** (Prijeko 12, tel: 020-321 599) also runs a variety of tours. For cruises, try **Gulliver Travel** (Obala S. Radića 32, tel: 020-313 313, www.gulliver.hr); and the **Adriana Shipping Company** (tel: 020-471 199; www.adriana.com.hr) does Elaphite Islands trips and others along the Dubrovnik Riviera (Lokrum, Mlini, Plat, Cavtat) on attractive old-style sailing boats.

OUTDOOR ACTIVITIES

Although Dubrovnik is principally a city destination, there are a number of sports and outdoor activities on offer – mostly on the water. Sea kayaking, rafting and canoeing are all popular. **Atlas Travel** *(see left)* organises 'Adventure tours', which include these activities and provide guides, instructors and equipment. They also do jeep safaris through the beautiful Konavle region (south of the city) and whole-day cycling tours on the island of Šipan. Sea kayaking in the bay between Fort Bokar and Fort Lovrijenac (just outside the city walls) is run by **Adventure Dalmatia** (tel/mobile: 091-526 3813, www.adventuredalmatia.com). Kayaking around Lokrum Island (with transfers from the city) is organised by **Adria Avanture** (tel: 020-332 567, www.adriaadventure.hr); and **Adriatic Kayak Tours** (tel: 020-312 770, www.adriatickayaktours.com), who also offer kayaking from Lopud to Šipan and cycling around Šipan.

You can water ski, or rent a speedboat, off Banje Beach; contact the **EastWest Club** (tel: 020-412 220).

Water polo is very popular in Dubrovnik (and particularly in Cavtat), but for visitors this tends to be a spectator rather than a participatory sport.

Above: enjoying the warm, clean waters off Dubrovnik

USEFUL ADDRESSES

Tourist Offices

The main tourist offices are in Branitelja Dubrovnika 7, just up from the Pile Gate (tel: 020-427 591), which is the most helpful; in Široka 7 (tel: 020-323 587), off Stradun; and Sv. Domnika 7 (020-312 011). There is another in Gruž, at Obala S. Radića 27 (tel: 020-417 983); and in Lapad, at Šetalište Kralja Zvonimira 25 (020-437 460). E-mail for information: info@tzdubrovnik.hr.

Consulates

UK: Buničeva Poljana 3, tel: 020-324 597, mobile: 091-455 5325.
The UK is the only English-speaking country with a consulate in Dubrovnik. Others have embassies in Zagreb, as follows:
USA: Thomasa Jefferson 2, Zagreb, tel: (385) 01-661 2300.
Australia: Kaptol Center, Nova Ves 11/3, 1000 Zagreb, tel: (385) 01-489 1200.
Canada: Prilaz Gjure Dezelica 4, 1000 Zagreb, tel: (385) 01-488 1200.

Croatian Consulates Abroad

UK: 21 Conway Street, London W1P 5HL, tel: 020-7387 2022; Visa Section: 7387 1144.
US: 2343 Massachusetts Avenue NW, Washington DC 20008, tel: 202-588 5899; 369 Lexington Avenue, New York, NY 10017, tel: 212-599 3066.
Australia: 14 Jindalee Crescent, O'Malley ACT, 2606, Canberra, tel: 2-6286 6988.
Canada: 229 Chapel Street, Ottawa, Ontario KIN 7Y6, tel: 613-562 7820.

Croatian Tourist Offices Abroad

UK: Croatian National Tourist Office (and Croatian Airlines), 2 The Lanchesters, 162–164 Fulham Palace Road, London W6 9ER, tel: 020-8563 7979.

USA: Croatian National Tourist Office, 350 Fifth Avenue, Suite 4003, New York, NY 10118, tel: 212-279 8672.

Useful Websites

www.croatia.hr
www.dubrovnik-online.com
www.webtourist.net

FURTHER READING

Berlitz Pocket Guide Croatia by Robin Mc-Kelvie, 2004 and *Berlitz Pocket Guide Dubrovnik* by Roger Williams, Berlitz/Apa Publications 2006. Succinct, useful guides to the country and city respectively.
Black Lamb and Grey Falcon by Rebecca West, Cannongate, 1993. Excellent, highly subjective account of Yugoslavia in the 1930s. Paperback.
Croatian Nights ed. Borivoj Radaković, Matt Thorne and Tony White, Serpent's Tail, 2005. A fine, eclectic collection of short stories by Croatian and British writers. It grew out of a movement called FAK – Festival of Alternative Literature – and gives an insight into how young writers look at the country. Paperback.
Dubrovnik: A History by Robin Harris, Saqi, 2003. A detailed, weighty, but accessible history of the city. Hardback.

Above: you get a sense of Dubrovnik's history from its old stone walls

ACKNOWLEDGEMENTS

Photography	**Glyn Genin/Apa** *and*
25	**Peter Adams/gettyimages**
32	**Dominican Convent, Dubrovnik/**
	Bridgeman Art Library
10	**Dominican Monastery, Dubrovnik**
64	**Korčula Museum**
30L	**Museum of Modern Art, Dubrovnik**
46, 52, 54, 60, 70, 71, 72	**Mark Read/Apa**
80	**Joel W. Rogers/Corbis**
12, 15	**TopFoto**
16	**UNEP/Milo Kovac/TopFoto**
5L	**Roger Williams**
2/3, 27T	**Gregory Wrona/Apa**
Cover	**SIME/Johanna Huber**

© APA Publications GmbH & Co. Verlag KG Singapore Branch, Singapore

INDEX

Accommodation 85–8
Akvarij (Aquarium) 36
Andrijić brothers 36, 62
antiques 69
Arboretum, Trsteno 58

Babin Kuk 42–3
Babine Kuce, Mljet 53
Banje beach 39
Blaise, St (Sveti Vlaho) 13, 21, 28
Bokar Fortress 23
Boškovića Square 37
Bošković, Ruder 37
Botanical Gardens, Lokrum 45
Božidarević, Nikola 32
Braće Andrijića 36
Branitelja Dubrovnika 24
Brown, Roland 30, 56
Bukovac, Vlaho 40
    Gallery 57

Calendar of Events 79
Cathedral 30
    Treasury 30
Cavtat 54–7
Chanson de Roland 27
churches
    Danče Church and Convent 24
    Dominikanska (Dominican Church
        and Monastery) 22, 32
    Franjevački Samostan (Franciscan
        Monastery Church), Cavtat 55
    Gospe od Karmena (Our Lady of
        Carmen) 36
    Gospa od Spilica (St Mary of Spilica),
        Lopud 49
    Sveti Ignacija (Jesuit Church) 22, 37
    Pravoslavne (Orthodox Church) 38
    Sveti Nikole (St Nicholas) Chapel 33
    Sveti Sebastijana (St Sebastian) 32
    Sveti Nikole (St Nicholas), Cavtat 55
    Sveti Petra (St Peter), Korčula 64
    Sveti Spas (Church of Our Saviour) 25
    Sveti Vlaho (St Blaise) 27–8
    Svih Svetih (All Saints), Korčula 64–5
City Walls 21–4
Clock Tower 27
clubs 77–8
communications 90
Congress of Vienna 14
consulates 92
Copacabana 43

Daksa island 43, 47
Dante Alighieri 24
Dobričević, Lovro 24, 26
Doge Pietro Orseolo II 11
Donje Čelo 47
Držića, Marin 38
Dubrovnik School 13
Dubrovnik Symphony Orchestra 29, 78
Dubrovnik University 24
Dulčić, Ivo 26, 28, 30

Earthquakes
    1667 (Great Earthquake) 13, 14, 22, 26
    1979 14, 36
eating out 71–6
Elephite Islands 47–50
embroidery 67

Ferdinand, Franz, Archduke 44
festivals
    general 79
    Moreska 64
    Return of Marco Polo (Korčula) 64
    St Blaise Festival 78–9
    Summer Festival 79
    Film Festival 79
food 68–9, 70–1
Fort Lovrijenac 23
Frana Bulića 24
Frana Supila 39
Franciscan Monastery 21, 25

Galerij Dulčić-Masle-Pulitika 30
Galerija Sebastian 32
Galija 53
Galileo 29
Getaldić, Marin 29, 40
Getaldić's cave 40, 41
Goddard, Wade 33
Gornje Čelo, Koločep 47
Gradac park 24
Gradska Kavana 28
Gradska Vijećnica (Town Hall) 28
Gradski Muzej, Korčula 62
Gruž 43
    Gruž Harbour 69
Gundulić, Ivan 26, 29, 37
Gundulić Square 31, 69

Hamzić, Mihajlo 30, 32
Hancez, Frederic 33
harbour 22

health 89
Hemingway Bar 30
history 11–17
Holocaust 33
Homeland War 15–6, 24
Holy Rosary Church 33
Hotel Belvedere 41
Hotel Excelsior 40
Hotel Odisej 53
Hungary 12–13
Hvar 50

Illiricum 11
Illyrian Movement 14
Internet Park 42

Jadrolinija ferrries 81
Jazz Caffé Troubador 31
Jesuit College 37
jewellery 67–8

Kamenica restaurant 31, 72
Knežev Dvor (Rector's Palace) 29
Koločep 47–8
Korčula 60–5
Kuća Marka Pola (Korčula) 64
Kuniceva restaurant 33

Lace 67
Lapad 42–3
Large Onofrian Fountain 25
Lazareti 22, 39, 78
Leut 55
Lindo Ensemble 39, 78
Lokanda Peskarija 28–9
Lokrum Island 22, 44–5
    monastery 45
Lopud 49–50
Luža Square 27, 31, 32

Madonna della Seggiola 30
Mali Most 53
Mali Ston 55
Malo Jezero (Small Lake) Mljet 53
Marco Polo 63–4
Marina, Korčula 65
Marin Držič Theatre 28
markets 31, 69
Masle, Antun 30
Mausolej Obiteliji Račić,
    Cavtat 55
Maximilian, Emperor of Mexico 44
Mea Culpa Restaurant 38

Memorial Room of the Defenders
    of Dubrovnik 27
Meštrović, Ivan 33
Michelozzi, Michelozzo 13, 29
Minčeta Fortress 21
Mljet 51–4
money 83
Morosini, Tommaso 12
Mount Srd 39, 41
Mrtvo More (Dead Sea) Lokrum 45
museums
    Dominican Monastery Museum 13, 32
    Dom Marina Držića (Home of Marin
        Držića) 38
    Etnografski Musej Rupe (Rupe Ethno
        graphic Museum) 38
    Franciscan Monastery Museum 25
    Icon Museum (Musej Pravoslavne
        Crkve) Dubrovnik 38–9
    Icon Museum, Korčula 65
    Maritime Museum (Pomorski Musej)
        22
    Museum of Modern Art (Umjetnička
        Galerija) 40
    Museum of the Homeland War 41
    Sinagoga Musej 33
    Treasury Museum, Korčula 62
music 78

National Park, Mljet 51
Nautika restaurant 23
nightlife 77 8

Od Puča 38
Old Port 28
Onofrio della Cava 25
Orebič 61
Orlando's Column 27
Orsan Yacht Club 43
Orthodox Church 38–9
Ottoman Empire 12–13
outdoor activities 91

Peace of Zadar 12
Pelješac peninsula 59
Pile Gate 21
Placa (see Stradun)
Plaža Sunj, Lopud 50
Ploče Gate 39
Ploče entrance (to City Walls) 22
Poklisar 28, 72
Polače 51
Pomena 53

Pozzo, Andrea 37
Pracat, Miho 29, 49, 50
Prijeko 33
Primorska Vrata, Korčula 61
Pristanište, Mljet 52
public holidays 84
Pulitika, Duro 30, 33

Radić, Stjepan 15
Ragusa II restaurant 33, 73
Rector's Palace 29
Rector's Palace, Cavtat 55
Republic of Ragusa 11
restaurants 71–6
Revelin Fortress 22, 39
Richard the Lionheart 30, 44
Ronald Brown Memorial House 30
Ronald Brown Trail, Cavtat 56

St Blaise 13
St Clare's Convent 25
St Cyril 11
St Jacob Monastery 41
St Mary's Island (Sveta Marija) 51, 52–3
St Methodius 11
shopping 67–9
Šipan 48
Šipanska Luka (Šipan) 49
Sloboda Cinema 28
Small Onofrian Fountain 27
Sobra, Mljet 51
Sponza Palace 27
Štalište Kralja Zvonimira 42
Stari Grad (Old Town) 25
Statue of Orlando (see Orlando's Column)
Stjepović-Skočibuha, Vice 48
Ston 59–60
Stradun 25–7, 31

Sudurad 48
Sunj Bay, Lopud 50
Sveti Ivan Fortress 22
Sveti Jakova 22
Sveti Margarita Fortress 22
Sveti Spasitelj Fortress 22
Sveti Stjepan Fortress 22
Svetoga Durda 23
Synagogue 33

Tito 15
tour agencies 91
tourist offices 92
Town Hall 28
Trsteno 58–9
Tudjman Bridge 47
Tudjman, Franjo 47

Ulysses Cave 54
Uvala Lapad (Lapad Bay) 42
Uvala Tiha, Cavtat 56
UNESCO World Heritage Site 5
Ustace Croatian Liberation Movement 15

Velika Kneževa Kula, Korčula 65
Veliko Jezero (Big Lake) Mljet 52
Veliki Ston 59
Venice 11–12
Villa Dubrovnik Hotel 40
Villa Koruna, Mali Ston 60
Villa Scheherazade 40

War Photo Limited 33
wine 68–9
World War II 15

Za Rokum 38
Zaton 58